Culturally Responsive
Lessons & Activities

Grade 6

All illustrations and photography, including those from Shutterstock.com, are protected by copyright.

Writing: Monika Davies
Content Editing: Lisa Vitarisi Mathews
Teera Robinson
Copy Editing: Kathleen Jorgensen
Art Direction: Yuki Meyer
Cover Design: Yuki Meyer
Illustration: Bryan Langdo
Design/Production: Paula Acojido
Yuki Meyer
Jessica Onken

EMC 8266

Visit *teaching-standards.com* to view a correlation of this book. This is a free service.

Correlated to Current Standards

Congratulations on your purchase of some of the finest teaching materials in the world.

Photocopying the pages in this book is permitted for <u>single-classroom use only</u>. Making photocopies for additional classes or schools is prohibited.

For information about other Evan-Moor products, call 1-800-777-4362, fax 1-800-777-4332, or visit our website, www.evan-moor.com. Entire contents © 2022 Evan-Moor Corporation 18 Lower Ragsdale Drive, Monterey, CA 93940-5746. Printed in USA.

CPSIA: Bradford & Bigelow, Newburyport, MA USA [12/2022]

Contents

Introduction

What's in *Culturally Responsive Lessons and Activities?* 4

How to Use This Book 6

About Culturally Responsive Teaching and Learning 7

Student Contents 8

How Do I Say It with Respect? 9

Sharing Forms 10

Units

Nonfiction and Informational Fiction

You Don't Have to Be Like Other People:
Lata Mangeshkar's Story 11

Be Determined to Overcome Hard Times:
Tyler Perry's Story 23

Let Your Heart Shine Through: Bethany Yellowtail's Story 35

A Great Attitude Can Lead to Opportunities:
Celina Smith's Story 47

Realistic Fiction

Be Proud of Your Creativity: We Love Hip-Hop Music! 59

You Can Be a Friend: Shanice, Holly, and Isabella 71

You Can Accept Changes and Still Be Yourself:
Zaina's Diary 83

Different Is Good: Celebrating New Experiences 95

Cultural Exploration and Self-Discovery

Let's Celebrate Who We Are 107

Food Is Part of Culture 119

Class Book 131

What's in *Culturally Responsive Lessons and Activities?*

8 Nonfiction, Informational Fiction, and Realistic Fiction Units

The units in this book are about people from diverse backgrounds with different abilities, ethnicities, and origins. Four units feature nonfiction biographical or informational fiction stories about people who are inspirational and perseverant. Four units feature realistic fiction stories about authentic situations and challenges that real people experience. Each unit has a different theme and begins with a teacher page that introduces the subject and activities. The story pages and activities are reproducible for students. The unit's theme is shown at the top of each student page.

Examples of themes include:

Different Is Good

Be Determined to Overcome Hard Times

You Can Accept Changes and Still Be Yourself

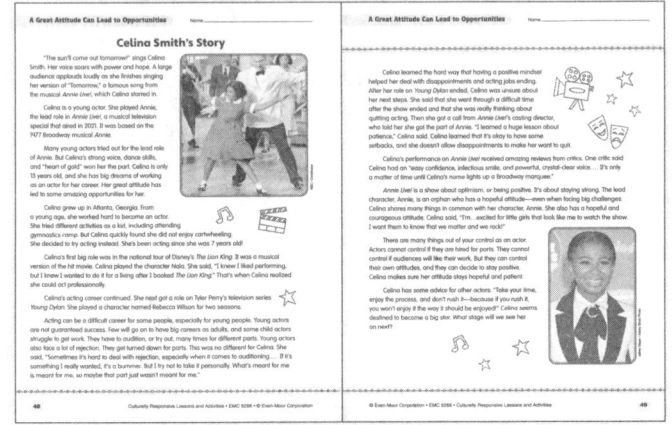

Story

Each of the nonfiction, informational fiction, and realistic fiction units has a reproducible two-page story that the subsequent activities relate to. The story emphasizes the unit's theme.

The stories describe real-life experiences in an age-appropriate way. They tell how people overcame challenges, navigated through complicated situations, and made choices that defined their lives. All of these story subjects and themes were chosen thoughtfully because of their power to inspire and the importance of representation.

Theme-Based Activities

Each unit has an activity that students complete independently, a whole-class or small-group discussion activity, a partner activity, and a project menu. Students choose from hands-on projects, performance projects, and creative writing projects.

Activities in all units vary and are designed to be engaging and open-ended, with a wide variety of response formats. The goal is for students to feel like the activities are providing a "safe space" to share their own unique viewpoints and experiences.

Activities include the following:
- creative writing and drawing
- critical thinking
- visual information
- discussion
- hypothetical scenarios and problem solving
- making choices and justifying opinions
- art projects

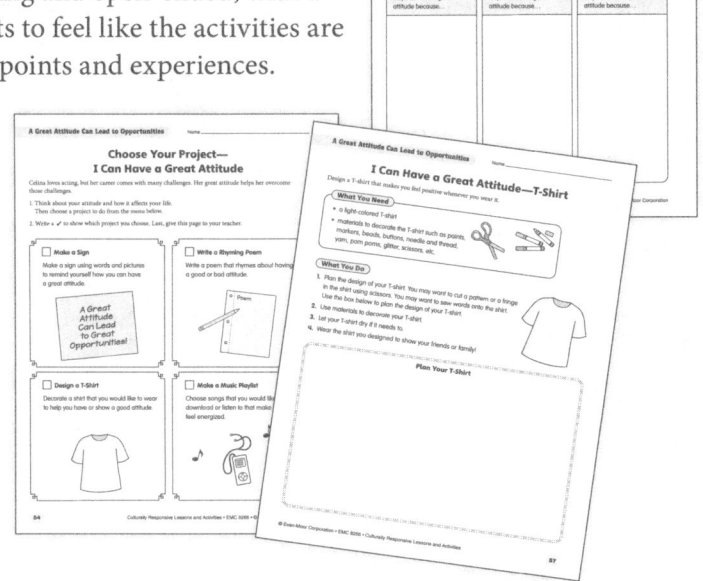

3 Cultural Exploration and Self-Discovery Units

The cultural exploration and self-discovery units are not centered around a text, rather they feature a variety of engaging and creative activities that invite students to reflect on their own cultures and interactions with the world. The activities prompt students to share about their own opinions, tastes, families, and experiences. These activities also support students in being culturally responsive by keeping an open mind, learning about the people around them with the intention of recognizing their value, and considering other viewpoints. Many of the activities provide opportunities for collaboration and whole-class projects. Some collaborative activities include making a class book, comparing handprints, and interviewing their classmates.

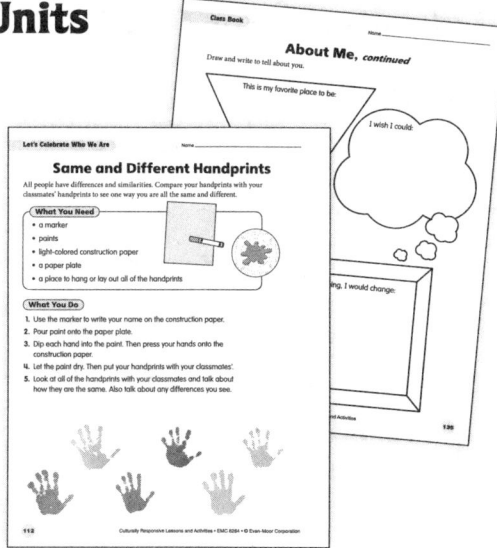

Student Resources

Additional pages provide students with support as well as opportunities for students to take an active role in their learning.

Student Contents

The Student Contents lists each unit title followed by a brief description of the featured person or theme. If you wish to allow students to choose which units they'd like to do based on their interests, reproduce and distribute the Student Contents to students.

How Do I Say It with Respect?

This page provides support for students as they participate in discussions. The statements and sentence starters emphasize respect for others and suggest what students might say if they agree, disagree, have a question, don't know what to say, or don't want to answer. You may wish to reproduce and distribute this page to students before you begin the first unit.

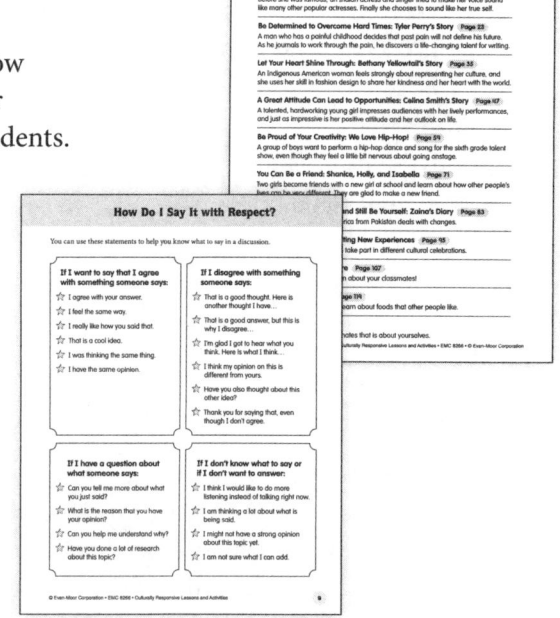

Student and Parent/Guardian Sharing Forms

The Student and Parent/Guardian Sharing Forms are intended to provide a connection between home and school. The purpose is to invite students and their families to communicate directly with the teacher and to take an active role in their learning.

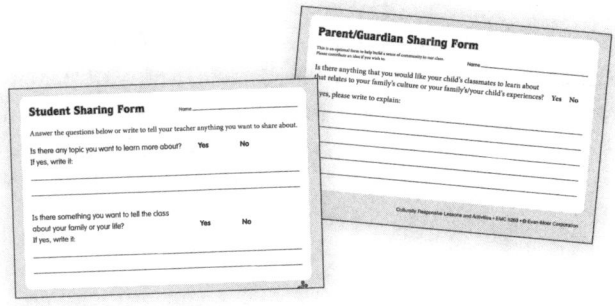

How to Use This Book

Planning Instruction

Nonfiction, Informational Fiction, and Realistic Fiction Units

Teacher Pages

Each unit begins with a teacher page that summarizes the focus of the unit and provides a suggested teaching path.

Nonfiction, Informational Fiction, and Realistic Fiction Stories

These units center around the story and theme, such as Hard Work Is a Common Language. The story provides context for the activities and projects. You can choose the activities that align with your students' needs or provide opportunities to increase engagement and positive interactions among students. Or you can allow students to choose the theme or person they would like to read about by reproducing the Student Contents on page 8 and distributing it to students.

Independent Activities

Each nonfiction, informational fiction, and realistic fiction story is followed by an independent activity that provides students opportunities to reflect on the story and the theme and relate it to their own lives.

Discussion Activities

Each unit includes a discussion activity. Before the discussion, students read the discussion items that are based on the story and theme. They are asked to think about their own opinions and experiences, and they may choose to write about them in preparation for the discussion. Before you begin the whole- and small-group discussions, you may wish to reproduce and distribute page 9, How Do I Say It with Respect? This page provides ideas and suggestions for statements and sentence starters that encourage respectful and productive communication.

Partner Activities

Each unit includes partner activities that are intended to help students learn about each other as they also learn more about themselves. To prepare for these activities, consider how you will assign partners or what process you will use to have students choose partners. It is important that students connect with classmates that they may not have in their social circle.

Choose Your Project Activities

Each unit includes a project menu for students to choose from. The project choices include hands-on, performance, and creative writing projects. Many of the projects require materials that are commonly part of classroom art supplies. Before you distribute the Choose Your Project activities to students, you may wish to confirm that you have access to the materials needed.

Cultural Exploration and Self-Discovery Units

Teacher Pages

Each unit begins with a teacher page that summarizes the focus of the unit and provides an overview of the activities and projects in the unit.

Activities, Games, and Projects

These units focus on learning about oneself and others through the lens of culture, family traditions, and peoples' similarities and differences. The activities, games, and projects range from individual to collaborative and often extend to home and family.

The pages in these units do not have to be completed in sequential order. Choose the activities that you want your students to complete, or offer them the opportunity to choose based on their interests.

About Culturally Responsive Teaching and Learning

Culturally responsive teaching is about connecting students' cultures and life experiences with what they are learning in school. Cultural responsiveness is creating a climate in which all students can feel a sense of belonging while also feeling safe to be their authentic selves as they process the curriculum and academic content.

These are some things you might see in a culturally responsive learning environment:

- Student-choice learning activities
- Students sharing about their home lives, first languages, or other cultural and personal experiences
- A sense of community as an emphasis during learning, in addition to academic content
- Family involvement in the learning process

Evan-Moor's Approach to Culturally Responsive Teaching and Learning

The activities in this book are designed to provide students with choices for how to demonstrate their learning and unique viewpoints. Many of the activities, including the group discussions, give students the opportunity to share about their own families and experiences. Our goal is to help students explore their own individualities, cultures, and life experiences and to help them learn more about their classmates, as well as to help teachers gain insights about who their students are so they can make every student's learning more meaningful. The authentic stories in this book represent people from many backgrounds and reflect the diversity and life experiences of people in our world. We hope these stories are both inspiring and enlightening for students.

Student Contents

You Don't Have to Be Like Other People: Lata Mangeshkar's Story Page 11
Before she was famous, an Indian actress and singer tried to make her voice sound like many other popular actresses. Finally she chooses to sound like her true self.

Be Determined to Overcome Hard Times: Tyler Perry's Story Page 23
A man who has a painful childhood decides that past pain will not define his future. As he journals to work through the pain, he discovers a life-changing talent for writing.

Let Your Heart Shine Through: Bethany Yellowtail's Story Page 35
An Indigenous American woman feels strongly about representing her culture, and she uses her skill in fashion design to share her kindness and her heart with the world.

A Great Attitude Can Lead to Opportunities: Celina Smith's Story Page 47
A talented, hardworking young girl impresses audiences with her lively performances, and just as impressive is her positive attitude and her outlook on life.

Be Proud of Your Creativity: We Love Hip-Hop! Page 59
A group of boys want to perform a hip-hop dance and song for the sixth-grade talent show, even though they feel a little bit nervous about going onstage.

You Can Be a Friend: Shanice, Holly, and Isabella Page 71
Two girls become friends with a new girl at school and learn about how other people's lives can be very different. They are glad to make a new friend.

You Can Accept Changes and Still Be Yourself: Zaina's Diary Page 83
A girl who immigrates to America from Pakistan deals with changes.

Different Is Good: Celebrating New Experiences Page 95
A boy and his mom choose to take part in different cultural celebrations.

Let's Celebrate Who We Are Page 107
Share about yourself and learn about your classmates!

Food Is Part of Culture Page 119
Tell about foods you like and learn about foods that other people like.

Class Book Page 131
Make a book with your classmates that is about yourselves.

How Do I Say It with Respect?

You can use these statements to help you know what to say in a discussion.

If I want to say that I agree with something someone says:

- ☆ I agree with your answer.
- ☆ I feel the same way.
- ☆ I really like how you said that.
- ☆ That is a cool idea.
- ☆ I was thinking the same thing.
- ☆ I have the same opinion.

If I disagree with something someone says:

- ☆ That is a good thought. Here is another thought I have…
- ☆ That is a good answer, but this is why I disagree…
- ☆ I'm glad I got to hear what you think. Here is what I think…
- ☆ I think my opinion on this is different from yours.
- ☆ Have you also thought about this other idea?
- ☆ Thank you for saying that, even though I don't agree.

If I have a question about what someone says:

- ☆ Can you tell me more about what you just said?
- ☆ What is the reason that you have your opinion?
- ☆ Can you help me understand why?
- ☆ Have you done a lot of research about this topic?

If I don't know what to say or if I don't want to answer:

- ☆ I think I would like to do more listening instead of talking right now.
- ☆ I am thinking a lot about what is being said.
- ☆ I might not have a strong opinion about this topic yet.
- ☆ I am not sure what I can add.

Student Sharing Form

Name _____

Answer the questions below or write to tell your teacher anything you want to share about.

Is there any topic you want to learn more about?   **Yes**   **No**
If yes, write it:

_____

_____

Is there something you want to tell the class
about your family or your life?   **Yes**   **No**
If yes, write it:

_____

_____

Parent/Guardian Sharing Form

This is an optional form to help build a sense of community in our class. Please contribute an idea if you wish to.

Name _____

Is there anything that you would like your child's classmates to learn about
that relates to your family's culture or your family's/your child's experiences?   **Yes**   **No**

If yes, please write to explain:

_____

_____

_____

_____

You Don't Have to Be Like Other People

Lata Mangeshkar's Story

This unit is about being yourself and knowing that you do not have to imitate other people to be successful. In fact, sometimes trying to be like others may prevent success. Students will read about Lata Mangeshkar, a woman with one of the most recognizable and unique singing voices in the world, who learned to accept the uniqueness of her voice. Students may already have experiences with choosing to be themselves or to be like others, so they may connect to Lata Mangeshkar's story, or they may learn how valuable it is to be unique. As you guide students through these topics, consider their varying world views as they share their experiences and make connections to their own lives.

The pages in this unit are reproducible. Reproduce the unit in its entirety or choose the pages that you wish to have your students do. A suggested teaching path is below.

1. **Read the Nonfiction Story (pages 12 and 13)**
   Distribute one copy of the text to each student. Have students read the text independently, or read the text aloud as they follow along silently.

2. **Being Unique (page 14)**
   Distribute one copy of the page to each student. Guide students in completing the page independently.

3. **Let's Talk About Lata Mangeshkar (page 15)**
   Distribute one copy of the page to each student. Facilitate a whole-group discussion or divide the class into small groups.

   Prepare for discussion:
   Tell students that they will have a conversation with classmates about the questions they have been given. Explain that they do not have to write complete answers to the questions. They can write notes about how they want to answer the questions or how they want to respond to other students' comments. Remind students that they can disagree with or add on to what other students say, as long as all students are respectful.

4. **Talk with Your Partner and Partner Time Opinion Cards (pages 16 and 17)**
   Divide students into groups of two. Distribute one copy of page 16 to each student. Distribute one copy of page 17 to each group. Have each group work on the activity together.

5. **Choose Your Project—You Are Unique (pages 18–22)**
   Distribute one copy of the project menu to each student. Explain to students that they will each choose a project to do. After students have chosen their project, collect the project menus.

   Reproduce and distribute one of the following project pages to each student based on the student's choice: Page 19 for the torn-paper picture; Page 20 for the handprint art; Page 21 for the collage; Page 22 for the song. Decide whether or not students will share their finished projects with the class and instruct students accordingly.

You Don't Have to Be Like Other People

Lata Mangeshkar has one of the most recognized singing voices in the entire world. Her voice is unique, unlike anyone else's. It has been recorded for hundreds of movies and thousands of songs during her long career. Even though she is famous for her one-of-a-kind voice, she did not always show her true voice to the world. For a long time she tried to sound like other singers because people told her it would be better.

In 1929, when Lata Mangeshkar was born, her father was a musical performer in India who wrote plays and stage shows. Lata received musical training from the age of 5 and acted in stage plays.

It is uncertain whether Lata ever attended school, but it is well known that she did not receive a traditional education. Sadly, her life changed when she was just 13 years old. That is when her father died of heart disease. Being the oldest sibling, Lata had to become the money earner for her entire family. She had to get a job even though she was still a child. It wasn't just a job that she could work at to make money for herself—she had to give the money to her family so they would have food and other things they needed to live. Lata had no choice. It was a lot of pressure for a 13-year-old.

Even though Lata is very famous today, she was not famous when she first started working. In the beginning, it was hard to find jobs. A family friend helped her get jobs acting in some Indian movies. She then tried to get work as a playback singer. A playback singer pre-records songs that will be used in movies. Lata went to studios where people recorded her singing. Sometimes her songs would not even be used in a movie at all. Playback singing work was not always available.

Sometimes it was difficult for Lata to get jobs. Many movie makers rejected her because they didn't like the sound of her voice. Some people said her voice was "too thin and sharp" to be in a movie. Lata's voice sounded very different from the style that was popular at the time. Movie makers wanted to hear a singing voice that sounded a certain way, and Lata's voice was different. Sometimes Lata tried to imitate, or copy, other well-known singers' voices to get hired.

You Don't Have to Be Like Other People

Lata was also criticized for her accent. So she started to learn Urdu, a different language, and she also tried to learn other accents and other styles of singing. She did all of this so that she could sound different from her true self. She thought she needed to sound like other people.

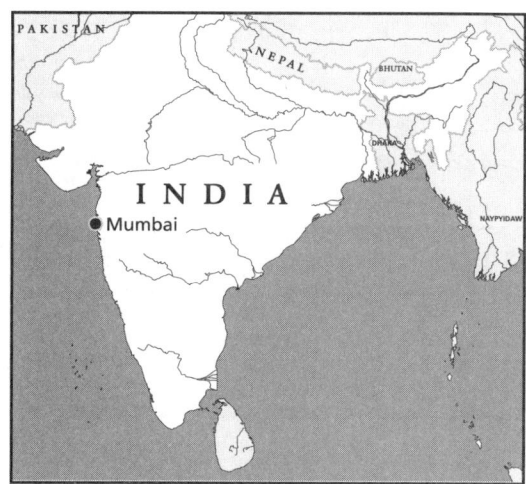

When Lata moved to Mumbai, she had more chances to find work. There was also more competition, though. This city is the center of Bollywood, the huge Indian filmmaking industry. After years of struggling and going from studio to studio, Lata recorded a playback song for a movie that was a huge hit. The song was called "Aayega Aanewala," and it was in the movie "Mahal" in 1949. And Lata used her real singing voice! Because this movie was a huge hit, Lata received many more jobs, and she continued to work as a playback singer for decades afterward, using her real voice.

In an interview, Lata said that she remembers the rough times when she would have to go hungry and when she had no money in her purse while looking for work. She said that those times were fun, even though she was struggling, because she always had hope in her heart.

During her career, Lata composed some of her own music and worked as a musical director for some films. But Lata is best known and most loved for being a playback singer, and that is because of her unique voice. If Lata Mangeshkar had only ever imitated other singers, perhaps the world would never have known her magical voice, which has made so many Bollywood movies memorable!

You Don't Have to Be Like Other People   Name _____

   # Being Unique

Lata Mangeshkar tried to imitate, or copy, other people's singing styles for a long time. She found true success when she decided to sound like herself.

Answer the items below about being unique.

1. Draw and write to tell one way that you are unique, or different, from everyone else.

   _____
   _____
   _____
   _____
   _____

2. Tell about a time when you tried to imitate someone else. Tell why you did it.

   _____
   _____
   _____
   _____

3. Draw a picture of yourself doing something that you like to do.

You Don't Have to Be Like Other People   Name _____

Let's Talk About Lata Mangeshkar

Read the questions. Think carefully about how to answer each one. You will talk with classmates about your ideas. There are no wrong answers. Below each question, you can write:

| Things that you want to say | Things other people said that you agree with | Things other people said that you disagree with |

1. Do you think that imitating other people is a good thing? Tell your opinion.

2. Lata Mangeshkar spent a lot of her time trying to learn new languages and accents because other people criticized her voice. Do you think people should ignore or listen to criticism from other people?

3. Do you think it was fair that Lata had to work as a child and give all the money she earned to her family? Tell why or why not.

4. Do you think you would try to imitate other people if it could help you make money?

You Don't Have to Be Like Other People

Name _____

  # Talk with Your Partner

Read the questions below and write your answers. Then talk with your partner about the answers you wrote.

1. Do you ever try to imitate people you see on TV or online? Tell about it.

2. What is one thing that makes your partner unique?

3. How do you feel when someone criticizes you?

4. If you had to get a job today to help earn money for your family, what kind of job would you want?

You Don't Have to Be Like Other People

Partner Time Opinion Cards

Everyone has an opinion and a point of view that makes them unique. Cut out the cards below and put them facedown in a pile. Pick a card and read it aloud. Tell your partner your opinion about what it says.

Opinion Card

It is cool to be unique because that is what makes you special and different from everyone else.

Opinion Card

It is hard to be unique because when you are different, you may feel left out, like you don't fit in.

Opinion Card

Sometimes you must be brave to be yourself because if people don't like you as you are, it can really hurt.

Opinion Card

It is okay if you don't know what makes you unique or what your special talent is. It takes time to find out.

Opinion Card

It is okay to try to be like other people. It may mean that you like things about those people.

Opinion Card

People deserve a chance to be themselves without being criticized.

You Don't Have to Be Like Other People

Name _____

Choose Your Project—
You Are Unique

Lata Mangeshkar realized that her uniqueness is what made her most successful and happy, and imitating other people did not make her as successful.

1. Think about the ways you are unique. Then choose a project to do from the menu below.

2. Write a ✓ to show which project you choose. Last, give this page to your teacher.

☐ **Make a Unique Torn-Paper Picture**

Tear pieces of colored paper and put them together to make shapes or pictures. Every torn-paper picture is unique!

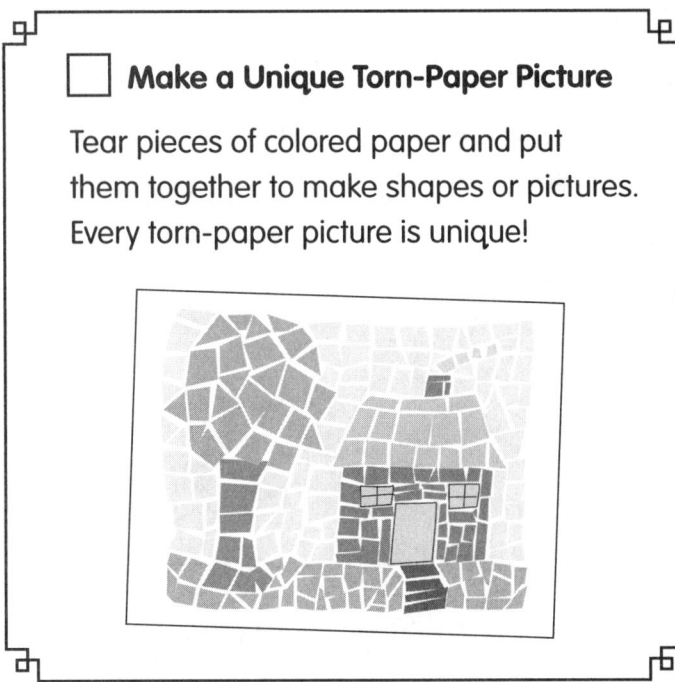

☐ **Make Handprint Art**

Make a handprint and write words on it to tell what makes you unique.

☐ **Make a Collage**

Cut and paste pictures and words on a poster to show your beliefs, your interests, and anything else you want to share about yourself.

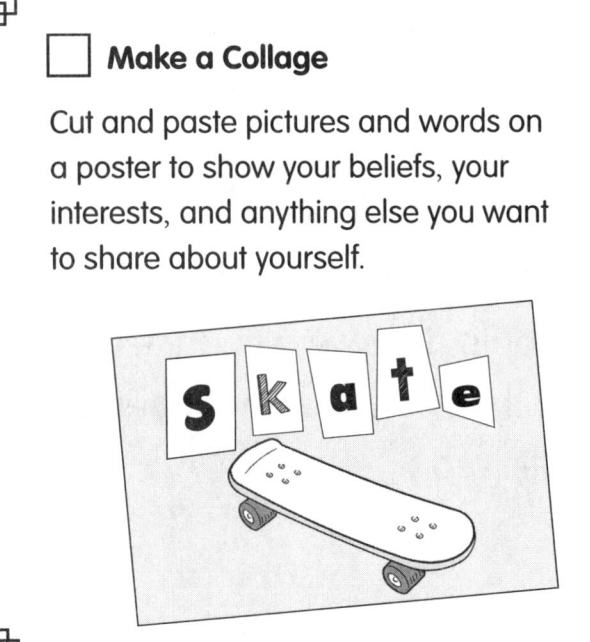

☐ **Write a Song**

Write song lyrics using the melody of a song you like. Write lyrics that tell about how you are unique.

You Don't Have to Be Like Other People

Name _____

You Are Unique—Torn-Paper Picture

Make a torn-paper picture that shows how unique and creative you are!

What You Need

- a sheet of construction paper or poster board
- sheets of colored construction paper
- glue or tape

What You Do

1. Tear the colored construction paper into pieces. Use the pieces to make a picture.
2. Glue or tape the torn pieces of paper onto the construction paper or poster board.
3. Hang your torn-paper picture somewhere.

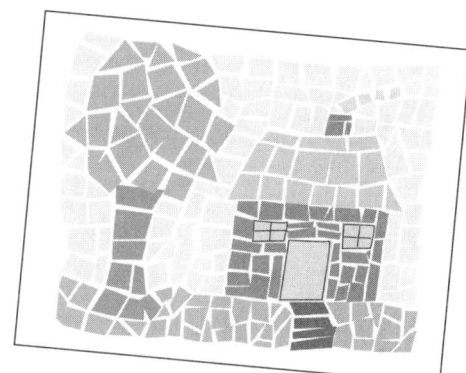

Plan Your Torn-Paper Picture

You Don't Have to Be Like Other People

Name _____

You Are Unique—Handprint Art

Make a handprint, and then write details on it about yourself.

What You Need

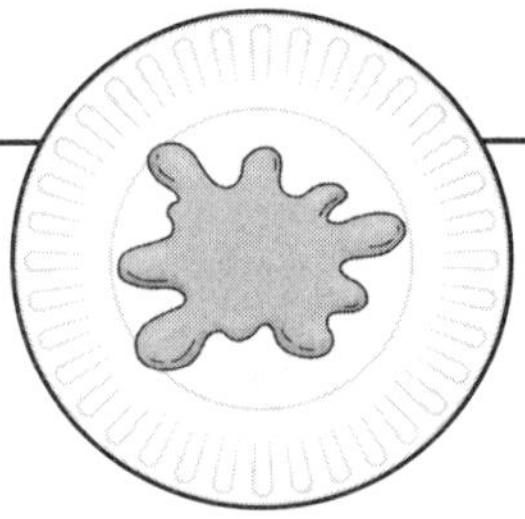

- light-colored paint
- a paper plate
- a sheet of light-colored construction paper
- crayons or markers

What You Do

1. Dip one hand into the paint, and then press it onto the construction paper.
2. Let the handprint dry.
3. On each finger, write one thing that makes you unique or different from other people.
4. On the palm of the handprint, write one adjective to describe yourself.
5. Show your handprint art to someone.

Plan Your Handprint Art

You Don't Have to Be Like Other People

Name _____

You Are Unique—Collage

Make a collage to show how unique you are. Cut and paste pictures or words to show what you believe, what you like, or anything else you want to share.

What You Need

- a sheet of colored construction paper
- scissors
- glue or tape
- magazines or papers with pictures and words that you can cut out
- materials to decorate a collage, such as markers, paint, glitter, cotton balls, foil, colored tissue paper, etc.

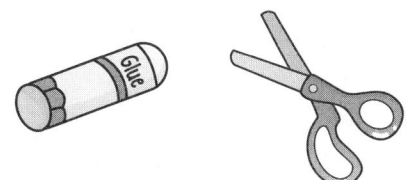

What You Do

1. Cut out pictures that represent you and things you like.
2. Glue or tape the pictures onto construction paper in any shape or arrangement you want.
3. Use other materials to decorate the construction paper.
4. Hang your collage on your bedroom door.

Plan Your Collage

You Don't Have to Be Like Other People

Name _____

You Are Unique—Song

Write song lyrics that tell about you!

What You Need
- a song of your choice to imitate
- a pen or pencil
- a smartphone or other device that can record audio

Think of a song with a tune that you would like to sing along to. Write a new title for the song. Then write words about you and what you believe, why you are special, what you like, or anything else about you to the tune of that song. After you finish writing the song, practice singing it. Then record yourself singing your song!

_____
song title

_____   _____
_____   _____
_____   _____
_____   _____
_____   _____
_____   _____
_____   _____
_____   _____
_____   _____

Be Determined to Overcome Hard Times

Tyler Perry's Story

This unit is about finding productive ways to overcome painful experiences so that they don't hold you back from having a happy future. Students will read about well-known actor Tyler Perry, who found out that journaling was a tool he could use to overcome pain in his life and discovered his skill for writing. Tyler Perry chose to help himself and to help others. Students may already have experiences with painful times, so they may relate to Tyler Perry's story, or they may learn anew that you can find ways to process pain. As you guide students through these topics, consider their varying world views as they share their experiences and make connections to their own lives.

The pages in this unit are reproducible. Reproduce the unit in its entirety or choose the pages that you wish to have your students do. A suggested teaching path is below.

1. **Read the Informational Fiction Story (pages 24 and 25)**
   Distribute one copy of the text to each student. Have students read the text independently, or read the text aloud as they follow along silently.

2. **Things I Can Try to Overcome (page 26)**
   Distribute one copy of the page to each student. Guide students in completing the page independently.

3. **Let's Talk About Tyler Perry (page 27)**
   Distribute one copy of the page to each student. Facilitate a whole-group discussion or divide the class into small groups.

   Prepare for discussion:
   Tell students that they will have a conversation with classmates about the questions they have been given. Explain that they do not have to write complete answers to the questions. They can write notes about how they want to answer the questions or how they want to respond to other students' comments. Remind students that they can disagree with or add on to what other students say, as long as all students are respectful.

4. **Talk with Your Partner and Partner Bookmark (pages 28 and 29)**
   Divide students into groups of two. Distribute one copy of each page to each group. Have each group work on the activity together.

5. **Choose Your Project—Getting Through Tough Times (pages 30–34)**
   Distribute one copy of the project menu to each student. Explain to students that they will each choose a project to do. After students have chosen their project, collect the project menus.

   Reproduce and distribute one of the following project pages to each student based on the student's choice: Page 31 for the playlist; Page 32 for the song; Page 33 for the journal entry; Page 34 for the dance. Decide whether or not students will share their finished projects with the class and instruct students accordingly.

© Evan-Moor Corporation • EMC 8266 • Culturally Responsive Lessons and Activities

Be Determined to Overcome Hard Times

Name _____

Tyler Perry's Story

As soon as the bell rang, Jameson grabbed his backpack and walked as fast as he could to where the school buses were parked. He knew he would get in trouble if he missed the bus again. His mom got mad the last time he had to call her from the school office to pick him up. She didn't like it when she had to leave work early.

When Jameson got off the bus, he walked around the block and used his key to get into his house. His grandpa was home in bed, as always, but he couldn't really take care of Jameson because he had Parkinson's disease. Jameson sometimes felt like he was home alone until his mom got home from work. He made sure Grandpa was comfortable and had water. Then he turned on the TV. He pulled some papers out of his backpack. "Hmm, I have to write a report about someone," he said to himself. Just then, he saw Tyler Perry on the television. "I'll write about Tyler Perry!" he decided.

Jameson went online and searched for information about Tyler Perry. He read an interview with Tyler in which he said he had a painful childhood. He also read that Tyler worked hard to deal with his painful memories. Some people may find it hard to feel happy after they have had a lot of pain in their lives. But Tyler chose to start writing a journal. He didn't want to let his painful memories stop him from living a full life and doing work that mattered to him. After Tyler started journaling, he felt a little better. He learned that a lot of the things that were bothering him were not his fault at all. This helped him put more energy into ideas for his work. He got an idea for a stage play, and he wrote it. Eventually, the play was performed onstage, and it sold out.

Tyler Perry wrote more plays, and the plays were so successful that they made millions of dollars. In 2006, Tyler created his own film production company, called Tyler Perry Studios. Finally, one of his plays was turned into a movie. After its success, Tyler Perry went on to make many more movies. He wrote and directed the movies, and he often acted in them, too.

 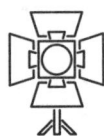 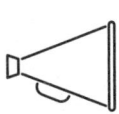    

Be Determined to Overcome Hard Times

"Wow," thought Jameson as he read. "Tyler Perry is such a famous star. I didn't know that he felt a lot of pain as a kid." Jameson thought about some of the struggles he had to go through sometimes. It was hard not always having his mom around because she had to work so much. Helping take care of his grandpa was difficult. He loved his Grandpa very much, yet he felt like he was all alone after school. And seeing his Grandpa with a disease also made Jameson feel sad. "My life isn't exactly how Tyler Perry's was," thought Jameson, "but I have some challenges in my life, too."

Jameson kept reading. He learned that Tyler Perry uses his money to help bring clean water to people who don't have enough in different countries such as Ethiopia and Cambodia. Tyler Perry also made the highest money donation ever made by a single person to the National Association for the Advancement of Colored People (NAACP). He donated 1 million dollars!

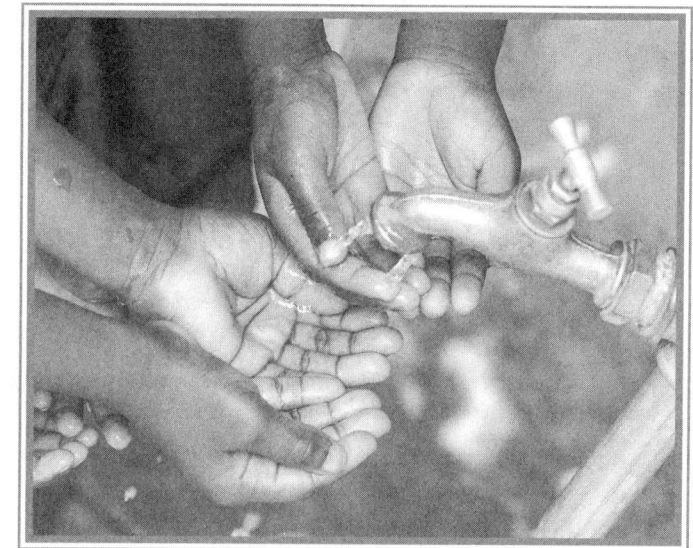

"I can't believe that somebody could be so unselfish," Jameson said to himself. "He had some really tough things happen to him, and then when he became rich and famous, it's like he couldn't wait to give some of his money away to help other people." Tyler Perry's generosity astonished Jameson. Then, a really interesting thought popped into Jameson's head. "Maybe I can do that one day. I want to help people."

Jameson spent most of the afternoon working on his report. Later, when his mom came home from work, Jameson told her lots of facts about Tyler Perry while she made dinner. She was tired, but she smiled and listened.

"I know things are tough for you too sometimes, Jameson," she said. "I'm so glad you are doing this report about Tyler Perry. It sounds like he is a very determined person. He didn't let past disappointments ruin his future."

After they ate their dinner, Jameson and his mom took dinner to Grandpa, and the small family spent some time together before bed.

Be Determined to Overcome Hard Times

Name _____

Things I Can Try to Overcome

Many people have things in their lives that they believe are good. And many people have things that they believe are hardships or that are painful. Everyone has some struggles. Even if we do not know what other people's struggles might be, we can try to remember that we all have them.

Think about things in your life that you consider to be hardships or that make your life a little bit harder. Answer the items below.

1. Write about one thing that you think makes your life a little harder or one thing you would change about your life if you could.

   _____

   _____

   _____

2. Tyler Perry found that journaling helped him put his pain aside so that he could focus on other things that brought him happiness. Journaling helped him learn that he was a good writer and develop ideas for a play. Draw a picture to show one thing you might be able to do to make use of your energy when you are feeling hardship or pain.

Be Determined to Overcome Hard Times

Name _____

Let's Talk About Tyler Perry

Read the questions. Think carefully about how to answer each one. You will talk with classmates about your ideas. There are no wrong answers. Below each question, you can write:

Things that you want to say  Things other people said that you agree with  Things other people said that you disagree with

1. Do you think that people can choose to move past hardships and not let the past stop them from reaching their dreams? Why or why not?

2. Why do you think Jameson felt connected to Tyler Perry's life story?

3. If a person believes that he or she has hardships, does it matter if other people agree or not? Do other people's opinions matter?

4. If you had success like Tyler Perry, would you donate a lot of your time or money to help other people? Why or why not?

Be Determined to Overcome Hard Times

Talk with Your Partner

Cut out the cards below. Each partner takes one. Write about a hardship that you face in your life that you can share with your partner, or write about a hardship that you have seen other people face. Then give your card to your partner to read. Last, talk about the hardships you and your partner wrote about.

Partner 1 One hardship that I face in my life or have seen:

_____

_____

_____

_____

_____

_____

Partner 2 One hardship that I face in my life or have seen:

_____

_____

_____

_____

_____

_____

Be Determined to Overcome Hard Times

Partner Bookmark

Sometimes we might feel like our problems are not as bad as other people's problems. At other times, we might feel like our problems are worse. It's important to remember that everyone might have problems and to respect the opinion of the person with the problem. It's up to that person to discover how he or she may be able to overcome his or her situation.

You talked with your partner about hardships. Cut out the bookmarks. Write or draw an inspirational picture or message on a bookmark to help your partner through hard times. Write your partner's name on the bookmark and give it to him or her.

For: _____

For: _____

Be Determined to Overcome Hard Times

Name _____

Choose Your Project—
Getting Through Tough Times

Tyler Perry found that journaling was a great way to get through tough times so he could focus on the future.

1. Think about some things that lift your mood and help you get through tough times. Then choose a project to do from the menu below.

2. Write a ✓ to show which project you choose. Last, give this page to your teacher.

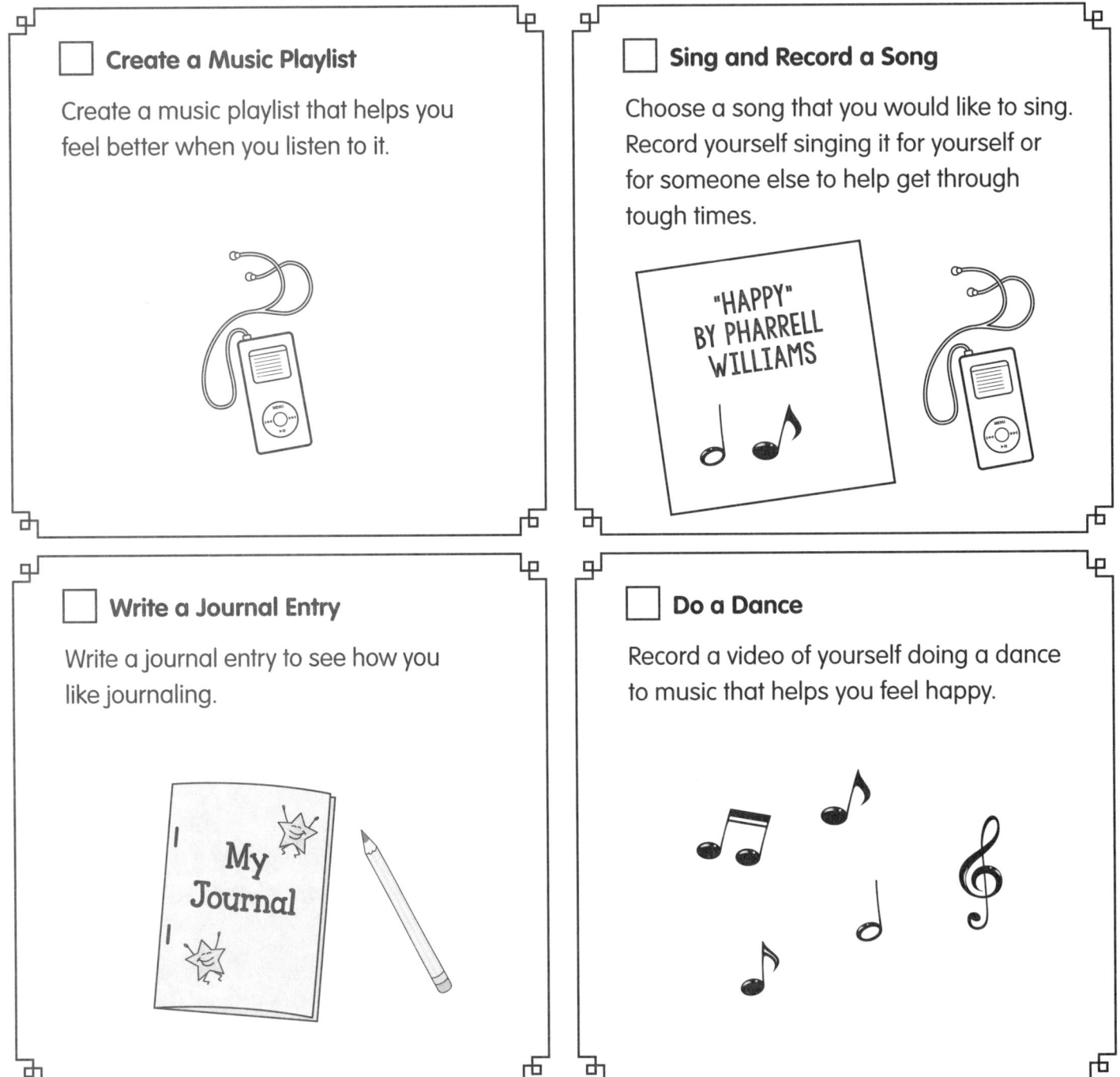

☐ **Create a Music Playlist**

Create a music playlist that helps you feel better when you listen to it.

☐ **Sing and Record a Song**

Choose a song that you would like to sing. Record yourself singing it for yourself or for someone else to help get through tough times.

"HAPPY" BY PHARRELL WILLIAMS

☐ **Write a Journal Entry**

Write a journal entry to see how you like journaling.

☐ **Do a Dance**

Record a video of yourself doing a dance to music that helps you feel happy.

Be Determined to Overcome Hard Times

Name _____

Getting Through Tough Times—Playlist

Make a music playlist with songs that help boost your mood.

What You Need

- smartphone or device that you can use to create a music playlist or pencil and paper

What You Do

1. Think of songs that put you in a good mood or make you feel supported.
2. Make a playlist of at least 5 songs. You can write your list on paper or make the list on your device.
3. Ask your parent if you can download the songs on your playlist or listen to them another way. Listen to them when you want to feel better.

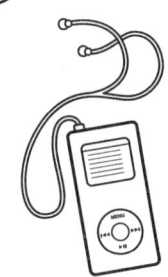

Plan Your Playlist

Be Determined to Overcome Hard Times

Name _____

Getting Through Tough Times—Song

Record yourself singing a song that helps you or someone else feel positive.

What You Need
- lyrics to a song, printed or written
- smartphone or device that can record audio

What You Do

1. Think of a song that you would like to sing.
2. Find the lyrics to the song and print them or write them.
3. Use a device to record yourself singing the song.
4. Listen to the recording to see if you like it. Re-record it if you want.
5. Play the recorded song for yourself or someone else.

Plan Your Song

Be Determined to Overcome Hard Times

Name _____

Getting Through Tough Times—Journal Entry

Write a journal entry to tell about your life and talk about any tough times you have had.

What You Need

- a sheet of lined paper
- a pen or pencil

What You Do

Write your own journal entry. You can use the questions below to help you if needed:

a. What do you like about yourself?
b. What is something good that has happend to you?
c. What is something difficult that you have experienced?
d. What helps you get through tough times?
e. What do you want to do in the future?

Plan Your Journal Entry

Be Determined to Overcome Hard Times

Name _____

Getting Through Tough Times—Dance

Record a dance video to get moving and help you feel positive.

What You Need

- a smartphone or other device for recording
- music to play and dance to
- an outfit or any props to use in your dance, such as a flag or a hat

What You Do

1. Think about songs that help you feel positive, and find a song to dance to.
2. Gather any props or put on any special clothing items that you want to wear in your dance.
3. You can use the box below to plan your steps or moves before you start dancing.
4. Record yourself dancing to the music or ask someone to help you record the video.
5. Show your dance video to friends or family.

Plan Your Dance

Let Your Heart Shine Through

Bethany Yellowtail's Story

This unit is about letting your heart shine through in your work and how that can lead to success. Students will read about Bethany Yellowtail, an Indigenous American fashion designer and the founder of B.Yellowtail, a notable fashion brand. Students may be thinking about following their hearts and going after their dreams, so they may connect to Bethany's story, or they might learn more about how to work, live, and give from the heart. As you guide students through these topics, consider their varying world views as they share their experiences and make connections to their own lives.

The pages in this unit are reproducible. Reproduce the unit in its entirety or choose the pages that you wish to have your students do. A suggested teaching path is below.

1. **Read the Nonfiction Story (pages 36 and 37)**
   Distribute one copy of the text to each student. Have students read the text independently, or read the text aloud as they follow along silently.

2. **In My Heart (page 38)**
   Distribute one copy of the page to each student. Guide students in completing the page independently.

3. **Let's Talk About Bethany Yellowtail (page 39)**
   Distribute one copy of the page to each student. Facilitate a whole-group discussion or divide the class into small groups.

   Prepare for discussion:
   Tell students that they will have a conversation with classmates about the questions they have been given. Explain that they do not have to write complete answers to the questions. They can write notes about how they want to answer the questions or how they want to respond to other students' comments. Remind students that they can disagree with or add on to what other students say, as long as all students are respectful.

4. **Talk with Your Partner and Permission Slips (pages 40 and 41)**
   Divide students into groups of two. Distribute one copy of page 40 to each student. Distribute one copy of page 41 to each group. Have each group work on the activity together.

5. **Choose Your Project—What I Care About (pages 42–46)**
   Distribute one copy of the project menu to each student. Explain to students that they will each choose a project to do. After students have chosen their project, collect the project menus.

   Reproduce and distribute one of the following project pages for each student based on the student's choice: Page 43 for the painting; Page 44 for the collage; Page 45 for the photo album; Page 46 for the dance. Decide whether or not students will share their finished projects with the class and instruct students accordingly.

Bethany's Story

Bethany Yellowtail is the Indigenous American founder and designer of B.Yellowtail, a fashion brand. Bethany's company sells clothes, handbags, jewelry, and much more.

Bethany grew up with fashion and community in her heart. She was raised in the Mighty Few District of the Crow Nation. That is in southeastern Montana.

As a kid, she'd sit with her sister in her Aunt Joy's living room. Her aunt shared cloth and materials with the two sisters. She taught them how to fringe their shawls. Bethany and her sister wore the shawls at their tribe's powwow. A powwow is a celebration at which Indigenous people gather to dance, sing, and honor their culture. Young Bethany's love for fashion was sewn together with her love for her culture and her community.

Her grandmother was the first to teach her how to sew. Growing up, Bethany spent hours sewing at her kitchen table. It was a part of her life at home. She later entered high school, where she took a home-economics class. "From the moment I sat down with a sewing machine in high school, I knew I found my calling," Bethany said. In her class, her teacher told her she had talent. Her teacher said Bethany could become a fashion designer. Bethany knew then that fashion design was her heart's calling.

One of Bethany's first designs was a bright pink blazer with matching pants. She made it for her high school leadership program. Beyoncé's look in the Pink Panther movie inspired Bethany's design. Bethany had already started turning heads with her fashion designs. After she graduated from high school, she moved to Los Angeles to keep developing her fashion career. The young designer went to college. She attended the Fashion Institute of Design & Merchandising.

After Bethany graduated, it was tough to find work. She worked at a local coffee shop for a year. Then she got a temporary job as a patternmaker at a fashion company called BCBG. Later, she got a full-time job at the company. Bethany spent her years at the company learning. She listened to top designers. She asked questions. She learned more about fabrics. But in her heart, Bethany knew her next career step.

Let Your Heart Shine Through

"I always knew I wanted to have my own brand," Bethany said. "The mission—leaving home and going to design school—was because I wanted to design my own clothes." In 2014, she launched her own brand called B.Yellowtail. Bethany wanted to see her culture represented in the fashion industry. She said, "I get to take all those parts of me that I love—the community I come from, the culture that I love, my family—and see it in B.Yellowtail."

There are special meanings for different colors or designs in Indigenous clothing. Bethany makes sure her brand creates clothes and other items with authentic Indigenous designs. "My homelands, the people I come from, and the cultural teachings I've been so fortunate to have learned have always informed my process," she said.

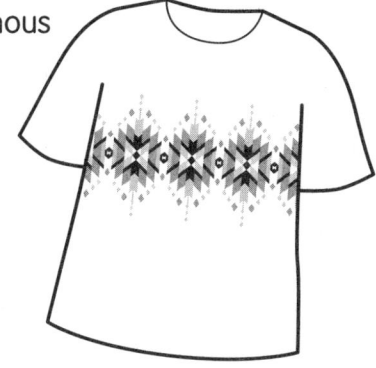

In 2016, she set up the B.Yellowtail Collective. This is an online shop on her website where other Indigenous American artists can sell their work. Bethany built this space to lift up other artists in her community. "There's a responsibility to give back to your people."

Bethany lives, gives, and works from her heart. Her culture and community is at the heart of who she is. She lets her heart shine through in her work. Bethany loves fashion. And she loves her culture and community. She intertwines these loves together in her work.

When Bethany was young, someone told her, "It doesn't matter where you come from… You deserve to dream and have the same opportunities as anyone else. You are allowed." Bethany gave herself permission to dream big. Some people did not believe she'd become a fashion designer. But Bethany knew this was her path. She knew this was her heart's calling. Now, she tells others, "Be fearless! You are capable!"

Let Your Heart Shine Through   Name _____

In My Heart

When your heart shines through, it means that you care deeply about what you choose to do. Bethany works and gives from her heart. Fashion is in her heart, too. Her community and culture also matter deeply to Bethany.

Answer the items below.

1. Draw or write to show what is in your heart, or what you care deeply about.

2. Explain why this is something you care deeply about.

_____

_____

_____

Let Your Heart Shine Through   Name _____

Let's Talk About Bethany Yellowtail

Read the questions. Think carefully about how to answer each one. You will talk with classmates about your ideas. There are no wrong answers. Below each question, you can write:

Things that you want to say    Things other people said that you agree with    Things other people said that you disagree with

1. Bethany's Indigenous culture guides and inspires her design work. How does your culture guide or inspire you?

2. What does it mean to "let your heart shine through" in your work? What does this phrase mean to you?

3. Bethany wanted to see her culture represented in fashion. Do you think it is important for many cultures to be represented where people work? Tell your opinion.

4. Giving back to her community is a big part of Bethany's life. Do you think giving back to our communities can help us do well in life?

© Evan-Moor Corporation • EMC 8266 • Culturally Responsive Lessons and Activities

Let Your Heart Shine Through

Name _____

·>>>·>>>·>>>·>>>·>>> Talk with Your Partner ·>>>·>>>·>>>·>>>·>>>

Read the questions below and write your answers. Then talk with your partner about the answers you wrote.

1. Do you have a heart's calling or big dream that you want to follow? Tell about it.

2. How do you think it would feel to be able to follow your big dream?

3. What is one thing that your partner does well and that you admire?

4. Who are the people in your heart? How can they help you follow your heart's calling?

Let Your Heart Shine Through

Permission Slips

Bethany gave herself permission to follow her heart, even when other people didn't believe she could do it. She wanted to become a fashion designer, and she made it happen. But it didn't happen right away for her. She gave herself permission to do other jobs and to keep trying to reach her big dream. What can you and your partner give yourselves permission for? Cut out the slips. Write on two slips to give yourself permission to do or be something. Your partner will do the same. Keep the slips.

Partner 1:
I can give myself permission to:
_____
_____
_____

Partner 1:
I can give myself permission to:
_____
_____
_____

Partner 2:
I can give myself permission to:
_____
_____
_____

Partner 2:
I can give myself permission to:
_____
_____
_____

Let Your Heart Shine Through

Name _____

Choose Your Project—
What I Care About

Bethany's heart shines through in her fashion designs. Her designs are made with love. They honor her culture and community. Think about what matters most to you and how you let your heart shine through in your life. Then choose a project to do from the menu below. Write a ✓ to show which project you choose. Last, give this page to your teacher.

☐ **Make a Painting**

Let your heart shine through! Paint a picture to show what matters most to you.

☐ **Make a Collage**

Cut and paste pictures and words on a poster to tell and show what is in your heart and matters most to you.

☐ **Make a Photo Album**

Make a photo album with photos that show what is in your heart and matters most to you.

☐ **Do a Dance**

Record a video of yourself doing a dance to music that is close to your heart.

Let Your Heart Shine Through

Name _____

What I Care About—Painting

Make a sign that shows how unique you are! You can use words, pictures, and symbols to show what you believe, what you are interested in, or anything else that you want to share!

What You Need

- a large sheet of construction paper
- paints
- paintbrush

What You Do

1. Use your paint and paintbrush to paint a picture of you doing something with people you love or doing an activity that is close to your heart. Maybe the painting can show you cooking a favorite dinner with your family.
2. Let your painting dry.
3. Hang your painting in your classroom or at your home.

Plan Your Painting

© Evan-Moor Corporation • EMC 8266 • Culturally Responsive Lessons and Activities

Let Your Heart Shine Through Name _____

What I Care About—Collage

Make a collage to show how unique you are. Cut and paste pictures or words to show what you believe, what you like, or anything else you want to share.

What You Need

- a sheet of colored construction paper
- scissors
- glue or tape
- magazines or papers with pictures and words that you can cut out
- materials to decorate a collage, such as markers, paint, glitter, cotton balls, foil, colored tissue paper, etc.

What You Do

1. Cut out pictures or words that represent what is in your heart and matters most to you.
2. Glue or tape the pictures onto construction paper in any shape or arrangement you want.
3. Use other materials to decorate the construction paper.
4. Hang your collage in your classroom or at home.

Plan Your Collage

Let Your Heart Shine Through

Name _____

What I Care About—Photo Album

Make a photo album with decorations, captions, or anything else you want to add to show your personality.

What You Need

- a smartphone or other device to take pictures
- a stapler
- 2 sheets of colored construction paper
- glue or tape
- materials to decorate the photo album cover, such as glitter, dried pasta, cotton balls, colored tissue paper, beads, buttons, foil, etc.

What You Do

1. Take photographs that show what is in your heart. Maybe the pictures can show your community or special parts of your culture. Make sure the pictures show what matters most to you.
2. Print the photographs.
3. Place the sheets of construction paper on top of each other and fold them in half like a book to make the photo album. Staple the paper together on the left side.
4. Glue or tape the photographs inside the photo album.
5. Decorate the cover of the photo album.

Plan Your Painting

Let Your Heart Shine Through

Name _____

What I Care About—Dance

Record a dance video that lets your heart shine through!

What You Need

- a smartphone or other device for recording
- music to play and dance to
- an outfit or any props to use in your dance, such as a flag or a hat

What You Do

1. Find a song to dance to.
2. Gather any props or put on any special clothing items that you want to wear in your dance.
3. You can use the box below to plan your steps or moves before you start dancing. Or you can just dance from your heart and make up the moves as you go. Remember to just let your heart shine through!
4. Record yourself dancing to the music or ask someone to help you record the video.
5. Show your dance video to friends or family.

Plan Your Dance

A Great Attitude Can Lead to Opportunities

Celina Smith's Story

This unit is about how having a great attitude can often help you overcome challenges and may also lead to future opportunities. Students will read about Celina Smith, a young rising star who played the lead character in the *Annie Live!* televised musical in 2021. Students might have their own big dreams, so they may connect to Celina's story, or they might learn how a positive attitude can help them persevere and reach their future goals. As you guide students through these topics, consider their varying world views as they share their experiences and make connections to their own lives.

The pages in this unit are reproducible. Reproduce the unit in its entirety or choose the pages that you wish to have your students do. A suggested teaching path is below.

1. **Read the Nonfiction Story (pages 48 and 49)**
   Distribute one copy of the text to each student. Have students read the text independently, or read the text aloud as they follow along silently.

2. **A Great Attitude (page 50)**
   Distribute one copy of the page to each student. Guide students in completing the page independently.

3. **Let's Talk About Celina Smith (page 51)**
   Distribute one copy of the page to each student. Facilitate a whole-group discussion or divide the class into small groups.

   Prepare for discussion:
   Tell students that they will have a conversation with classmates about the questions they have been given. Explain that they do not have to write complete answers to the questions. They can write notes about how they want to answer the questions or how they want to respond to other students' comments. Remind students that they can disagree with or add on to what other students say, as long as all students are respectful.

4. **Talk with Your Partner and Choosing Our Attitude (pages 52 and 53)**
   Divide students into groups of two. Distribute one copy of each page to each group. Have each group work on the activity together.

5. **Choose Your Project—I Can Have a Great Attitude (pages 54–58)**
   Distribute one copy of the project menu to each student. Explain to students that they will each choose a project to do. After students have chosen their project, collect the project menus.

   Reproduce and distribute one of the following project pages for each student based on the student's choice: Page 55 for the sign; Page 56 for the poem; Page 57 for the T-shirt; Page 58 for the playlist. Decide whether or not students will share their finished projects with the class and instruct students accordingly.

A Great Attitude Can Lead to Opportunities

Name _____

Celina Smith's Story

"The sun'll come out tomorrow!" sings Celina Smith. Her voice soars with power and hope. A large audience applauds loudly as she finishes singing her version of "Tomorrow," a famous song from the musical *Annie Live!*, which Celina starred in.

Celina is a young actor. She played Annie, the lead role in *Annie Live!*, a musical television special that aired in 2021. It was based on the 1977 Broadway musical *Annie*.

Many young actors tried out for the lead role of Annie. But Celina's strong voice, dance skills, and "heart of gold" won her the part. Celina is only 13 years old, and she has big dreams of working as an actor for her career. Her great attitude has led to some amazing opportunities for her.

Celina grew up in Atlanta, Georgia. From a young age, she worked hard to become an actor. She tried different activities as a kid, including attending gymnastics camp. But Celina quickly found she did not enjoy cartwheeling. She decided to try acting instead. She's been acting since she was 7 years old!

Celina's first big role was in the national tour of Disney's *The Lion King*. It was a musical version of the hit movie. Celina played the character Nala. She said, "I knew I liked performing, but I knew I wanted to do it for a living after I booked *The Lion King*." That's when Celina realized she could act professionally.

Celina's acting career continued. She next got a role on Tyler Perry's television series *Young Dylan*. She played a character named Rebecca Wilson for two seasons.

Acting can be a difficult career for some people, especially for young people. Young actors are not guaranteed success. Few will go on to have big careers as adults, and some child actors struggle to get work. They have to audition, or try out, many times for different parts. Young actors also face a lot of rejection. They get turned down for parts. This was no different for Celina. She said, "Sometimes it's hard to deal with rejection, especially when it comes to auditioning…. If it's something I really wanted, it's a bummer. But I try not to take it personally. What's meant for me is meant for me, so maybe that part just wasn't meant for me."

A Great Attitude Can Lead to Opportunities

Celina learned the hard way that having a positive mindset helped her deal with disappointments and acting jobs ending. After her role on *Young Dylan* ended, Celina was unsure about her next steps. She said that she went through a difficult time after the show ended and that she was really thinking about quitting acting. Then she got a call from *Annie Live!*'s casting director, who told her she got the part of Annie. "I learned a huge lesson about patience," Celina said. Celina learned that it's okay to have some setbacks, and she doesn't allow disappointments to make her want to quit.

Celina's performance on *Annie Live!* received amazing reviews from critics. One critic said Celina had an "easy confidence, infectious smile, and powerful, crystal-clear voice.... It's only a matter of time until Celina's name lights up a Broadway marquee."

Annie Live! is a show about optimism, or being positive. It's about staying strong. The lead character, Annie, is an orphan who has a hopeful attitude—even when facing big challenges. Celina shares many things in common with her character, Annie. She also has a hopeful and courageous attitude. Celina said, "I'm…excited for little girls that look like me to watch the show. I want them to know that we matter and we rock!"

There are many things out of your control as an actor. Actors cannot control if they are hired for parts. They cannot control if audiences will like their work. But they can control their own attitudes, and they can decide to stay positive. Celina makes sure her attitude stays hopeful and patient.

Celina has some advice for other actors: "Take your time, enjoy the process, and don't rush it—because if you rush it, you won't enjoy it the way it should be enjoyed!" Celina seems destined to become a big star. What stage will we see her on next?

A Great Attitude Can Lead to Opportunities

Name _____

A Great Attitude

Your attitude is how you think and feel about something. Celina has a hopeful attitude. She makes her dreams come true with patience and hard work.

Answer the items below about a great attitude.

1. Draw and write to tell about one way you try to have a great attitude.

   _____
   _____
   _____
   _____
   _____

2. Tell about a time when you did not have the best attitude. How did you feel and why?

   _____
   _____
   _____
   _____

3. Draw a picture of yourself doing something that helps you improve your attitude when you're feeling disappointed.

A Great Attitude Can Lead to Opportunities

Name _____

Let's Talk About Celina Smith

Read the questions. Think carefully about how to answer each one. You will talk with classmates about your ideas. There are no wrong answers. Below each question, you can write:

Things that you want to say Things other people said that you agree with Things other people said that you disagree with

1. Young actors face many challenges, such as rejection for acting roles. Why do you think rejection causes such painful feelings for some people?

2. Celina practices patience. Do you think patience is an important quality for a person to have? Tell why or why not.

3. Do you think your attitude is something you can control and change? Or is it something you cannot change?

4. Celina said that people should try to "enjoy the process" when trying to reach a goal. This means that people should try to enjoy the hard work and the time before they reach their goal. Do you agree with this idea?

A Great Attitude Can Lead to Opportunities

Name _____

Name _____

Talk with Your Partner

Celina's great attitude has led to great opportunities. Read the phrases in the "What Makes a Great Attitude?" box. Discuss them with your partner.

What Makes a Great Attitude?

| Being patient | Enjoying the process | Believing in yourself |
| Being hopeful | Being okay with making mistakes | Being kind to others |

1. Choose 3 phrases from the box above.
2. Write each phrase on the lines in the boxes below.
3. Then write to tell why each phrase helps you have a great attitude.

_____ helps us have a great attitude because…

_____ helps us have a great attitude because…

_____ helps us have a great attitude because…

52   Culturally Responsive Lessons and Activities • EMC 8266 • © Evan-Moor Corporation

A Great Attitude Can Lead to Opportunities

Name _____

Name _____

Choosing Our Attitude

What you choose to say and believe affects your attitude. You can choose your words. Your words can change your attitude. Talk with your partner about the sentences below. Then write different sentences you can choose to say instead.

I don't deserve to have that. →

I'll never be as talented as other people. →

This is too hard. I should give up. →

I'm scared of making mistakes. I don't want to try hard and then fail. →

A Great Attitude Can Lead to Opportunities   Name _____

Choose Your Project—
I Can Have a Great Attitude

Celina loves acting, but her career comes with many challenges. Her great attitude helps her overcome those challenges.

1. Think about your attitude and how it affects your life. Then choose a project to do from the menu below.

2. Write a ✓ to show which project you choose. Last, give this page to your teacher.

☐ **Make a Sign**

Make a sign using words and pictures to remind yourself how you can have a great attitude.

A Great Attitude Can Lead to Great Opportunities!

☐ **Write a Rhyming Poem**

Write a poem that rhymes about having a good or bad attitude.

☐ **Design a T-Shirt**

Decorate a shirt that you would like to wear to help you have or show a good attitude.

☐ **Make a Music Playlist**

Choose songs that you would like to download or listen to that make you feel energized.

A Great Attitude Can Lead to Opportunities Name _____

I Can Have a Great Attitude—Sign

Make a sign that shows your great attitude! You can use words, pictures, and symbols to show what a great attitude looks like, how you feel about challenges, or anything else that you want to share.

What You Need

- a large piece of poster board
- markers or crayons
- scissors
- glue or tape
- materials to decorate the sign, such as dried noodles, colored tissue paper, glitter, stickers, magazine cut-outs, paint

What You Do

1. Using large letters, write a statement, phrase, or question that tells why attitude is important.
2. Decorate the sign.
3. Hang or set up the sign in your classroom or at your home.

Plan Your Sign

A Great Attitude Can Lead to Opportunities

Name _____

I Can Have a Great Attitude—Poem

Write a rhyming poem that is all about attitude. Then record yourself reciting the poem.

What You Need

- a smartphone or other device to record sounds
- a pencil
- a sheet of lined paper

What You Do

1. Write a poem that rhymes and that is about attitude. Your poem can have any rhyming pattern.
2. Record yourself reading the poem aloud.
3. Play the recording for someone!

Plan Your Poem

A Great Attitude Can Lead to Opportunities

Name _____

I Can Have a Great Attitude—T-Shirt

Design a T-shirt that makes you feel positive whenever you wear it.

What You Need

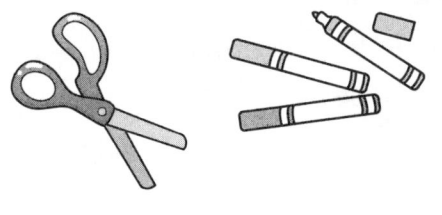

- a light-colored T-shirt
- materials to decorate the T-shirt such as paints, markers, beads, buttons, needle and thread, yarn, pom poms, glitter, scissors, etc.

What You Do

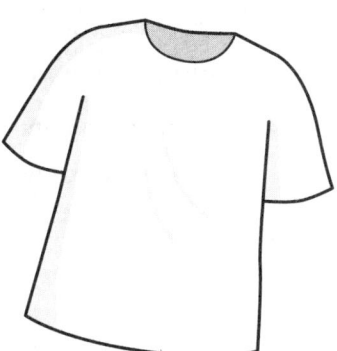

1. Plan the design of your T-shirt. You may want to cut a pattern or a fringe in the shirt using scissors. You may want to sew words onto the shirt. Use the box below to plan the design of your T-shirt.
2. Use materials to decorate your T-shirt.
3. Let your T-shirt dry if it needs to.
4. Wear the shirt you designed to show your friends or family!

Plan Your T-Shirt

A Great Attitude Can Lead to Opportunities

Name _____

I Can Have A Great Attitude—Playlist

Make a music playlist with songs that help you have a positive attitude.

What You Need

- smartphone or device that you can use to create a music playlist or pencil and paper

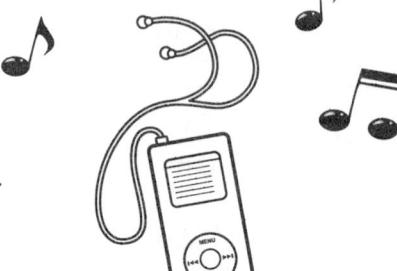

What You Do

1. Think of songs that make you feel capable, powerful, or energized.
2. Make a playlist of at least 5 songs. You can write your list on paper or make the list on your device.
3. Ask your parent if you can download the songs on your playlist or listen to them another way. Listen to them when you want to improve your attitude.

Plan Your Playlist

Be Proud of Your Creativity

We Love Hip-Hop Music!

This unit is about being proud of your creativity. Students will read a realistic fiction story about Diego, Jamal, and Nolan, three boys who want to show their hip-hop skills at their school's talent show. Students may have experienced nervousness about expressing their creativity in the past, so they may connect to the story, or they might learn the value of letting go of fear and showing their creative skills with pride. As you guide students through these topics, consider their varying world views as they share their experiences and make connections to their own lives.

The pages in this unit are reproducible. Reproduce the unit in its entirety, or choose the pages that you wish to have your students do. A suggested teaching path is below.

1. **Read the Realistic Fiction Story (pages 60 and 61)**
   Distribute one copy of the text to each student. Have students read the text independently, or read the text aloud as they follow along silently.

2. **Being Creative (page 62)**
   Distribute one copy of the page to each student. Guide students in completing the page independently.

3. **Let's Talk About the Story (page 63)**
   Distribute one copy of the page to each student. Facilitate a whole-group discussion or divide the class into small groups.

   Prepare for discussion:
   Tell students that they will have a conversation with classmates about the questions they have been given. Explain that they do not have to write complete answers to the questions. They can write notes about how they want to answer the questions or how they want to respond to other students' comments. Remind students that they can disagree with or add on to what other students say, as long as all students are respectful.

4. **Talk with Your Partner and Talent Show Partner Activity (pages 64 and 65)**
   Divide students into groups of two. Distribute one copy of each page to each group. Have each group work on the activity together.

5. **Choose Your Project Menu—Express Your Creativity (pages 66–70)**
   Distribute one copy of the project menu to each student. Explain to students that they will each choose a project to do. After students have chosen their project, collect the project menus.

   Reproduce and distribute one of the following project pages for each student based on the student's choice: Page 66 for the comic strip; Page 68 for the short story; Page 69 for the meal; Page 70 for the hip-hop song. Decide whether or not students will share their finished projects with the class and instruct students accordingly.

Be Proud of Your Creativity

Name _____

We Love Hip-Hop Music!

Diego, Jamal, and Nolan love listening to hip-hop on the radio. They know the lyrics to all their favorite songs. The three boys have been listening to rap and hip-hop since they were in 1st grade!

One day, Diego walked into school and saw a sign for the talent show. It said in big, bold letters, "Join us for Pine Street Elementary's Annual Talent Show!"

Diego's brain began churning with ideas. He loved being creative. Diego turned to his two best pals. "Guys, what if we did our *own* hip-hop song at the talent show?" he said. Diego could already see it in his mind. He knew he was a great rapper because he raps all the time at home! Nolan had sick dance moves. And Jamal could spit rhymes like nobody else.

"Dude, we've never written a song before," said Nolan. "Everyone will just laugh at us."

Jamal frowned, too. "No one else gets hip-hop like we do. Nobody in class will like it."

But Diego was no quitter. "But that's the point!" he said. "Nobody else gets hip-hop like we do—so we can show them how great it is. Everyone will see why it takes skill to do hip-hop right. Remember how Mr. McCloud told us the talent show is a chance to express our creativity? Hip-hop is our way of expressing ourselves! We can write our own song and figure out our own dance moves." Diego could tell he was persuading his friends. "Come on, guys," Diego pressed again. "I know we can do this. We got each other. Don't let fear hold us back."

Nolan and Jamal looked at each other. They both laughed. Jamal said, "I mean, I've always wanted to try freestyling."

"Yes!" Diego pumped his fist into the air, and his friends laughed again.

Be Proud of Your Creativity

Name _____

The three guys got together every day after school. The talent show was coming up soon, so they had to move fast. They debated back and forth. Should they freestyle? What rhythm did they want to use? How many lines did they need?

Nolan said he didn't want to rap but that he could dance. He started watching lots of music videos to get ideas for dance moves. Jamal started writing some rhymes, and Diego started putting together Jamal's rhymes into a 16-line song.

Diego wanted to do a good job. He knew that some of his classmates didn't really listen to rap music. He wanted them to like it.

The three boys practiced tirelessly, and soon the day of the talent show came. They found out their time slot, and they had to wait backstage until it was their turn to perform. They watched other kids go onstage. The other kids were doing lots of different kinds of performances. One girl played her flute. A 4th grader did card tricks! Another girl painted a picture in front of the audience.

Finally, it was time for Diego, Jamal, and Nolan to take the stage. The beat for their song started. Diego could feel his heart beating loudly in his chest. When he heard his cue, he just started rapping. Then Jamal started rapping his lines. Nolan went all out with the dance moves beside them. He even did his favorite dance move—the pop and lock. As they performed, the crowd was loving it. Nobody was laughing at them, but a lot of people were smiling! Some people were moving to the beat, too.

When they finished their song, they heard thunderous applause from the whole room. A few of the adults even whistled! Diego, Jamal, and Nolan took a deep bow and skipped off the stage, laughing and fist bumping. They did it, and they didn't let their fears stop them! They were so proud of themselves.

Be Proud of Your Creativity

Name _____

Being Creative

You can express your creativity in many ways. Diego and his friends wrote a hip-hop song. They also made up a dance. This was how they expressed their creativity. Write and draw to tell 3 ways you express creativity in your life.

This is one way I express my creativity at school:

_____

_____

_____

This is one way I express my creativity at home:

_____

_____

_____

This is one way I express my creativity with my friends:

_____

_____

_____

Be Proud of Your Creativity

Name _____

Let's Talk About the Story

Read the questions. Think carefully about how to answer each one. You will talk with classmates about your ideas. There are no wrong answers. Below each question, you can write:

Things that you want to say  Things other people said that you agree with Things other people said that you disagree with

1. Do you think it was right for Diego to keep pushing Nolan and Jamal to perform in the talent show when they didn't want to at first? Tell your opinion.

2. Do you think that people should give different or new kinds of music a try? Why or why not?

3. Do you think that doing something like performing even when you're nervous can help someone gain confidence? Why or why not?

4. Do you think music can become an important part of your identity, like it is for Diego? Tell your opinion.

Be Proud of Your Creativity

Name _____

Name _____

Talk with Your Partner

Everyone has creative skills! Nolan has dance skills. Diego has rapping skills. Other kids have musical skills, painting skills, and other skills. Talk with your partner about your creative skills or talents. Draw or write down your creative skills in the boxes below.

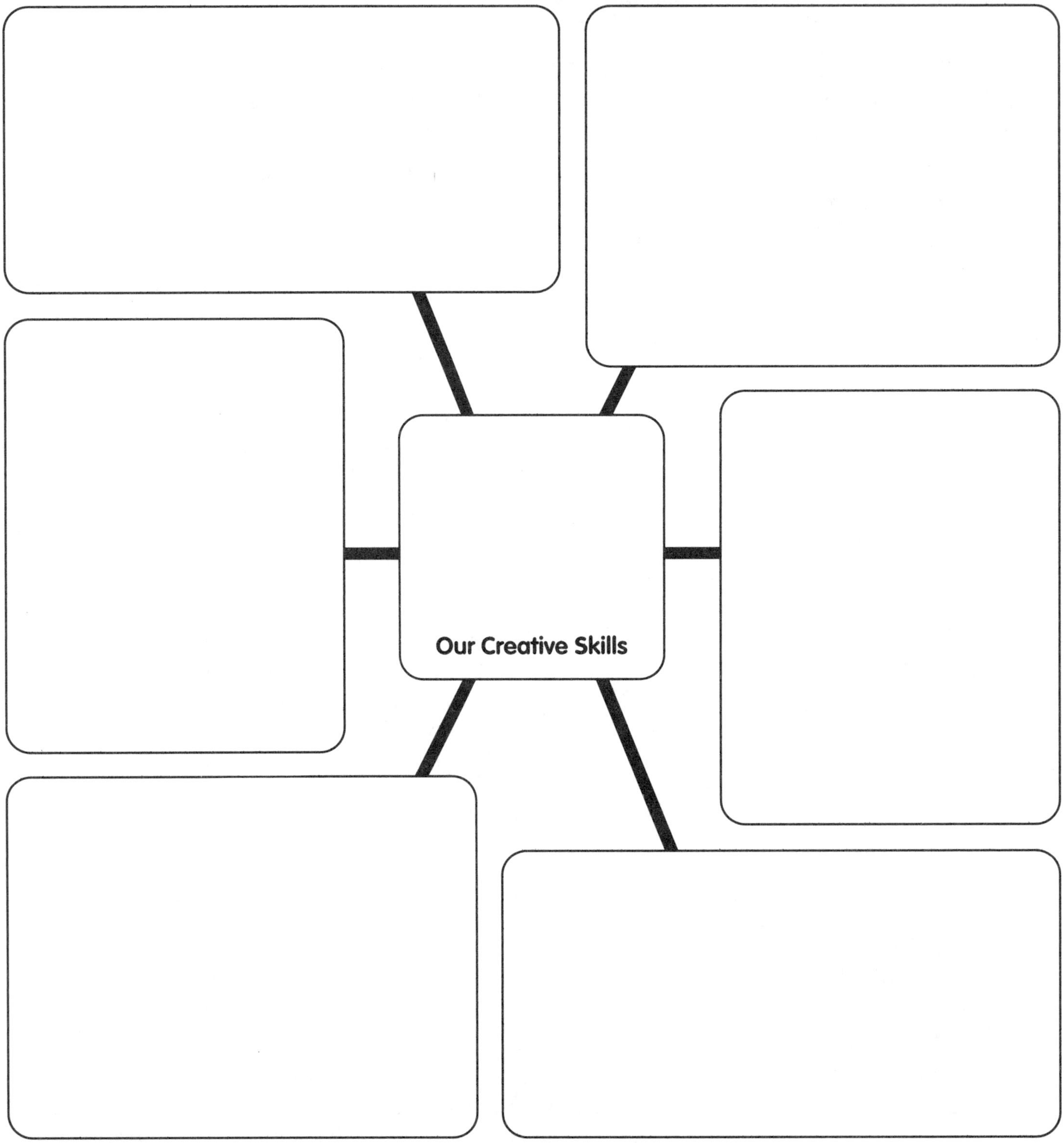

Our Creative Skills

Be Proud of Your Creativity

Name _____

Name _____

Talent Show Partner Activity

Be proud of your creativity! If you and your partner were in a talent show together, what would you do for your performance? Draw and write to tell how you and your partner would express your creativity together in a talent show.

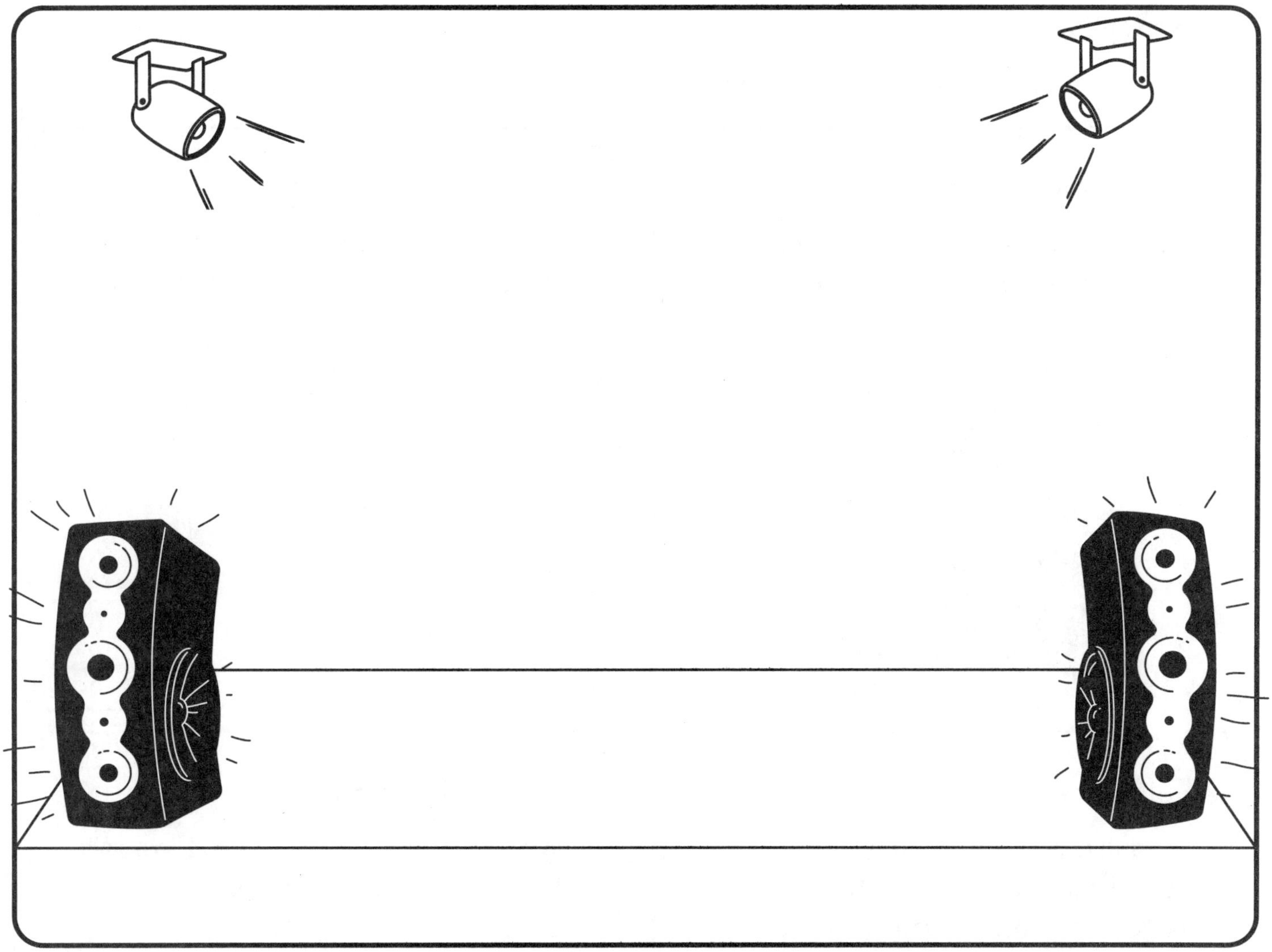

_____
_____
_____
_____
_____

Be Proud of Your Creativity

Name _____

Choose Your Project—
Express Your Creativity

Diego, Jamal, and Nolan showed their hip-hop skills at the talent show. Others showed painting skills and other forms of entertainment.

1. Think about your skills and how you can show your creativity. Then choose a project to do from the menu below.

2. Write a ✓ to show which project you choose. Last, give this page to your teacher.

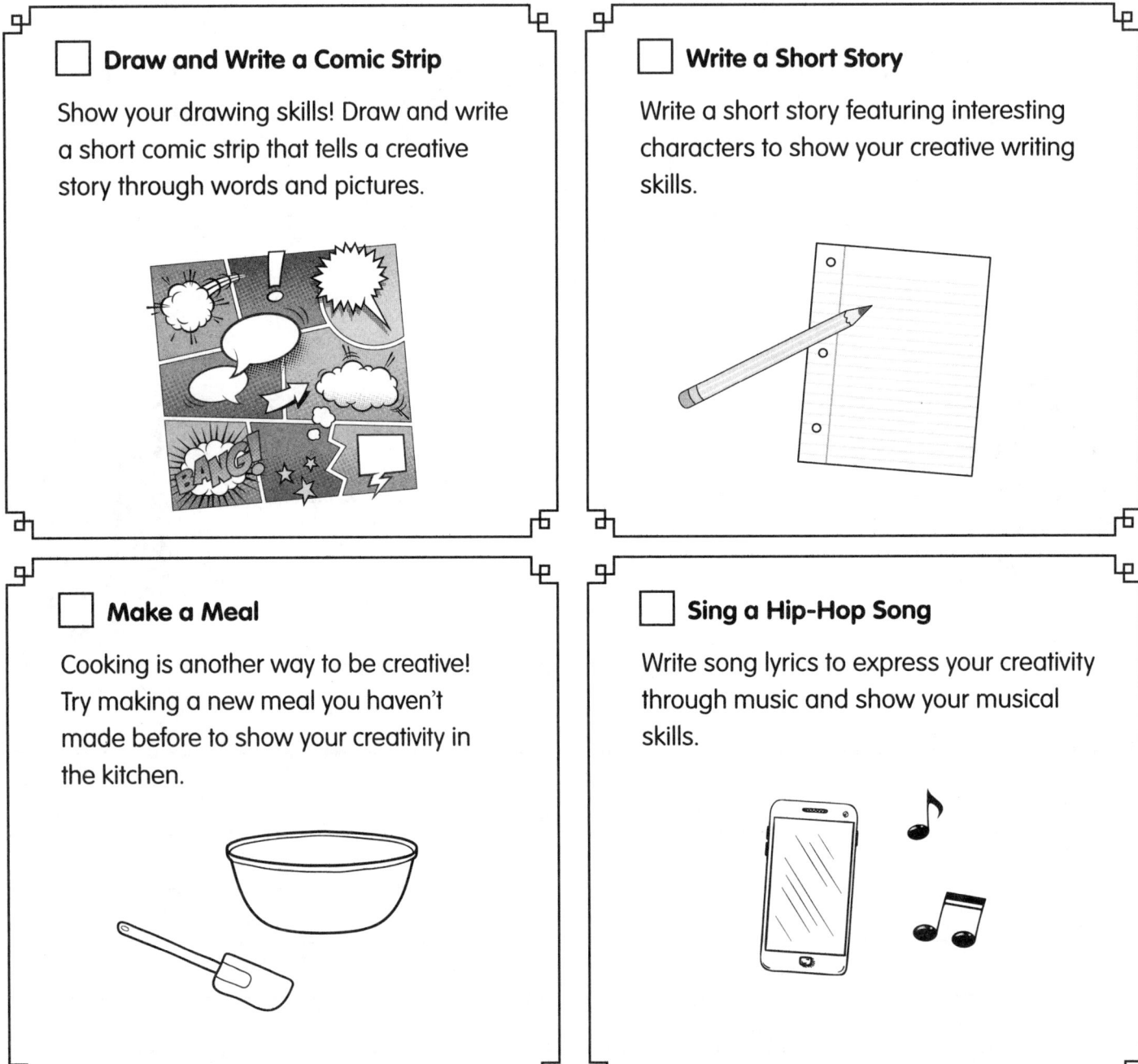

☐ **Draw and Write a Comic Strip**

Show your drawing skills! Draw and write a short comic strip that tells a creative story through words and pictures.

☐ **Write a Short Story**

Write a short story featuring interesting characters to show your creative writing skills.

☐ **Make a Meal**

Cooking is another way to be creative! Try making a new meal you haven't made before to show your creativity in the kitchen.

☐ **Sing a Hip-Hop Song**

Write song lyrics to express your creativity through music and show your musical skills.

Be Proud of Your Creativity

Name _____

Express Your Creativity—Comic Strip

Draw and write a comic strip to tell a creative story through words and pictures.

What You Need

- a large sheet of light-colored construction paper
- crayons or markers
- a sheet of lined paper
- pen or pencil
- ruler

What You Do

1. Write your story idea for your comic strip. A comic strip uses pictures and words to tell a short story through dialogue and sounds. Inside each shape is a different scene or part of the story.
2. Draw shapes for your comic strip on the construction paper.
3. Draw your story's characters or settings inside the shapes. Then draw speech bubbles. Write in each speech bubble to show what your characters are saying.
4. Color your comic strip using crayons or markers.
5. Share your comic strip with your friends or family.

Plan Your Comic Strip

Be Proud of Your Creativity

Name _____

Express Your Creativity—Short Story

Write a short story with an interesting character to show your creative writing skills.

What You Need

- a sheet of lined paper
- pen or pencil

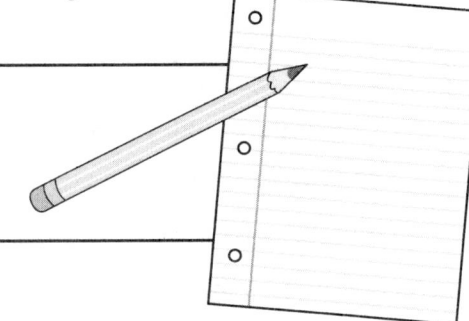

What You Do

1. You can write your own short story. Use the questions below to help you get started if needed:
    a. Who is the main character in your story?
    b. What does your main character want?
    c. What challenges will your character face to get what he or she wants?
    d. How will your character overcome his or her challenges?
2. Write your short story.
3. Share your short story with your friends or family.

Plan Your Short Story

Be Proud of Your Creativity

Name _____

Express Your Creativity—Meal

Make a new recipe to show your creative skills in the kitchen!

What You Need

- a recipe
- kitchen supplies needed for the recipe, such as bowls, measuring cups, mixing spoons, etc.
- a smartphone or other device to take pictures

What You Do

1. Find a new recipe you would like to try.
2. Ask an adult to help you in the kitchen.
3. Make the recipe and take a photograph of yourself making it.
4. Eat the food you made. Then show the picture to your friends.

Plan Your Meal

Be Proud of Your Creativity

Name _____

Express Your Creativity—Hip-Hop Song

Write lyrics for a hip-hop song to express your creativity and show your musical skills!

What You Need

- a song of your choice to imitate
- a smartphone or other device that can record audio
- a sheet of paper
- a pen or pencil

Think of a hip-hop song that you would like to sing along to. Write a new title for the song. Then write words that express your creativity and that go with that song. After you finish writing the song, practice singing it. Then record yourself singing your song!

Plan Your Song

You Can Be a Friend

Shanice, Holly, and Isabella

This unit is about the importance of reaching out and being friends with others, even though sometimes it is difficult to do when a person leads a life that is different from yours. Students will read about Shanice and Holly, two young students who befriend Isabella, the daughter of migrant farm workers who move around a lot. The girls are glad that they reached out and made a new friend. Students may know people who could use a friend, so they may connect to the story, or they might learn how everyone needs friends. As you guide students through these topics, consider their varying world views as they share their experiences and make connections to their own lives.

The pages in this unit are reproducible. Reproduce the unit in its entirety or choose the pages that you wish to have your students do. A suggested teaching path is below.

1. **Read the Realistic Fiction Story (pages 72 and 73)**
   Distribute one copy of the text to each student. Have students read the text independently, or read the text aloud as they follow along silently.

2. **Being a Friend (page 74)**
   Distribute one copy of the page to each student. Guide students in completing the page independently.

3. **Let's Talk About the Story (page 75)**
   Distribute one copy of the page to each student. Facilitate a whole-group discussion or divide the class into small groups.

   Prepare for discussion:
   Tell students that they will have a conversation with classmates about the questions they have been given. Explain that they do not have to write complete answers to the questions. They can write notes about how they want to answer the questions or how they want to respond to other students' comments. Remind students that they can disagree with or add on to what other students say, as long as all students are respectful.

4. **Talk with Your Partner and Partner Time Question Cards (pages 76 and 77)**
   Divide students into groups of two. Distribute one copy of the page to each group. Have each group work on the activity together.

5. **Choose Your Project—I Can Be a Friend (pages 78–82)**
   Distribute one copy of the project menu to each student. Explain to students that they will each choose a project to do. After students have chosen their project, collect the project menus.

   Reproduce and distribute one of the following project pages to each student based on the student's choice: Page 79 for the survey questions; Page 80 for the invitation; Page 81 for the collage; Page 82 for the journal entry. Decide whether or not students will share their finished projects with the class and instruct students accordingly.

You Can Be a Friend Name _____

Shanice, Holly, and Isabella

Holly and Shanice had been best friends since 2nd grade. They sometimes hung out with other people, but they were almost always together.

One day, the two girls sat in their usual spot in the cafeteria. Holly usually ate noodles while Shanice usually had a sandwich. As she was looking around, Shanice spotted a girl sitting across the room, someone she'd never seen before. "Who's the girl eating lunch alone?" Shanice asked, nudging her friend.

Holly looked up, squinting her eyes. "I've never seen her before." She frowned. "Maybe she's a new student?"

Shanice noticed that the girl was drawing and doodling in her notebook. Shanice loved to draw, too. Holly was more into taking photographs. "Should we say hi to her?" Shanice asked.

Holly looked surprised. "I don't know," she said, "maybe that girl wants to sit alone."

Shanice looked at the girl closer. "Well, it won't hurt to ask her," Shanice said. She thought that the girl looked kind of sad. Nobody else was talking to her or even looking at her.

At recess, Holly and Shanice hung out by the swing set. They took turns swinging. Then Shanice saw the same girl from lunch. She was sitting alone on a bench, and she had her notebook out again. "Everyone can use a friend," Shanice said to Holly. This time, Shanice decided to say hi. She walked over and said, "What are you drawing?"

The girl looked up. "I'm drawing different kinds of fruits. But I can't get this cherry to look right."

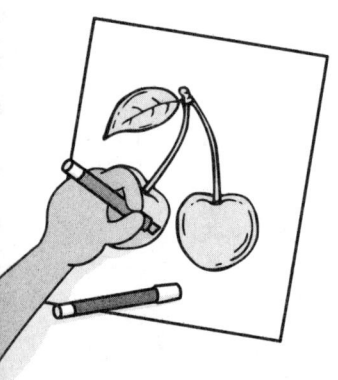

Holly came up beside them. She looked at the girl's drawing and whistled softly. "Whoa, that looks like I could pluck it and eat it right off the page." The girl shrugged.

Just then, the bell rang, and all the kids on the playground went inside the school. The next day, Shanice and Holly saw the girl again in the cafeteria. They asked her to sit with them.

"Sure," the girl said shyly. "I'm Isabella, by the way."

You Can Be a Friend

For the next month, Isabella sat with Holly and Shanice. They swapped stories from their classes, and the three learned more about each other. Holly talked about her fights with her younger sister. Shanice talked about her struggles to figure out ratios in math class. And Isabella talked about her family and where they came from.

"My parents work on the farms nearby," she said one day. "They help pick cherries. They're paid for every pound they pick."

"Is that tough work? It has to be tiring, right?" Holly says.

"Yeah, it's not easy. They get up early. During harvest season, they work seven days a week." Isabella pushed her rice around in her lunch container. "I also have to move a lot. That's tough, too. Every year, we move to several different states. We are originally from Mexico, but we have not been there for a long time. I go to at least three different schools every year."

It was hard for Holly and Shanice to imagine Isabella's life. Both their dads worked from home. And Holly and Shanice had never moved. In fact, they both lived in the same houses their entire lives.

"I never knew farm workers had to move around so much," Shanice said softly. "That sounds really difficult. It must be hard to make friends when you go to different schools every year."

"It can be tough," Isabella said. "My parents work really hard and I know they are doing the best they can."

Isabella told her new friends that she would have to move again in a couple of months. As the moving day got closer, Shanice and Holly started to feel really sad. They told Isabella that they would miss her a lot.

"We can keep in touch through e-mail, if you want to," said Isabella. The girls gave each other their e-mail addresses.

On Isabella's last day at the school, Shanice and Holly gave Isabella a hug. "We got this for you—just something to remember us by," Holly said. She handed Isabella a card. Inside was a photograph of the three of them.

Isabella smiled. "I'll keep this picture forever," she said. "Thanks for saying hi to me that day on the playground," she said. "You guys are the best friends I've ever had."

The next day, Holly and Shanice were sad that Isabella wasn't at school. But they knew they'd talk to her again soon. She was their friend!

You Can Be a Friend   Name _____

Being a Friend

Shanice and Holly reached out to Isabella. They listened to stories from her life and spent time getting to know her better. They became Isabella's friend.

Answer the items below about being a friend.

1. Draw and write to tell about one way that you are a friend to others.

   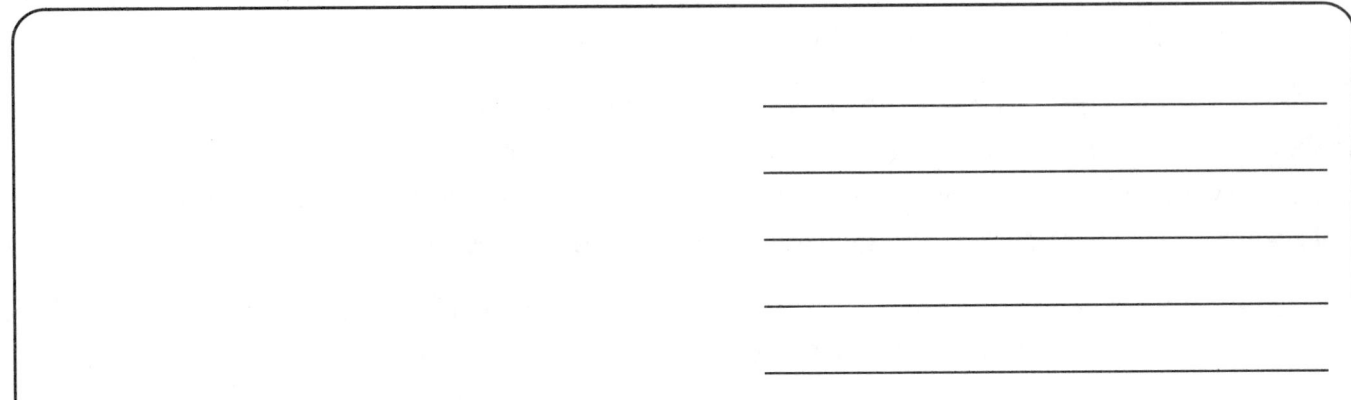

2. Describe one way that you would try to make new friends.

   _____
   _____
   _____
   _____

3. Shanice and Holly are friends who listen. Draw or write to tell 3 other qualities that are important in a friend.

   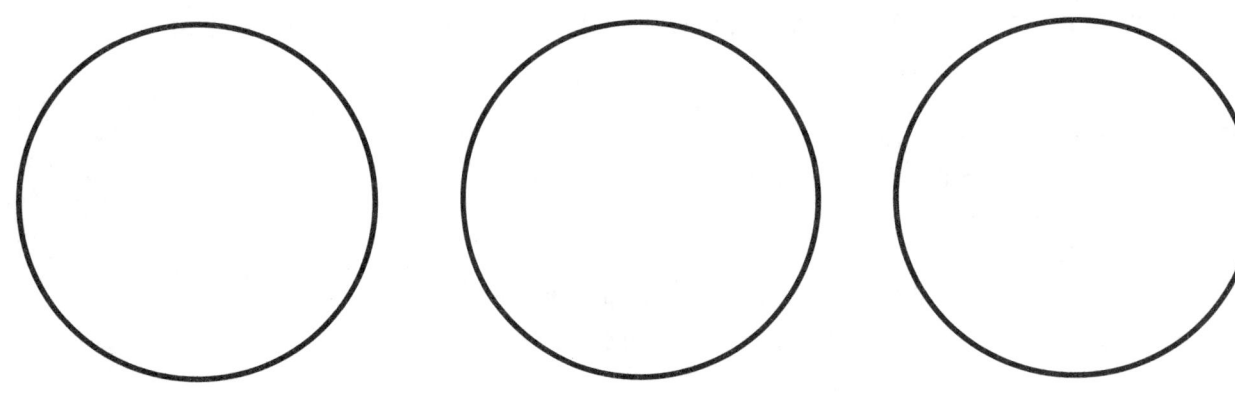

You Can Be a Friend

Name _____

Let's Talk About the Story

Read the questions. Think carefully about how to answer each one. You will talk with classmates about your ideas. There are no wrong answers. Below each question, you can write:

Things that you want to say  Things other people said that you agree with  Things other people said that you disagree with

1. Isabella was sitting alone when Holly and Shanice decided to say hi and ask her questions. Do you think it's easy or difficult to start talking to someone new?

2. Holly and Shanice were sad when Isabella had to move. Do you think it's possible to become friends with someone after only a few months? Why or why not?

3. Do you agree with Shanice that "everyone can use a friend"? Why or why not?

4. Do you think it's important to learn about other people's lives? Why or why not?

You Can Be a Friend

Name _____

Name _____

 ## Talk with Your Partner

Holly, Shanice, and Isabella became good friends over the school year. Think about what makes a good friend. Talk with your partner to brainstorm ideas. Draw or write all of your answers in the boxes below.

Good friends say...

What makes a good friend?

Actions of a good friend

You Can Be a Friend

Partner Time Question Cards

All people have stories to share about their lives. Cut out the cards below and put them facedown in a pile. Take turns picking a card and asking your partner the question aloud. Listen to your partner's answer carefully.

Question Card
What kind of music do you like the most? Why?

Question Card
What is one of your biggest fears?

Question Card
What is your favorite memory with your family?

Question Card
What is something that you find challenging or that you struggle to do?

Question Card
Which is your favorite meal: breakfast, lunch, dinner, or dessert? Why?

Question Card
How do you think your life will be different in five years?

Question Card
What is something not many people know about you?

Question Card
If you could change one thing in the world, what would you change?

You Can Be a Friend

Name _____

Choose Your Project—
I Can Be a Friend

Having friends made a big difference in Isabella's life.

1. Think about what makes a good friend and how you can be a friend. Then choose a project to do from the menu below.

2. Write a ✓ to show which project you choose. Last, give this page to your teacher.

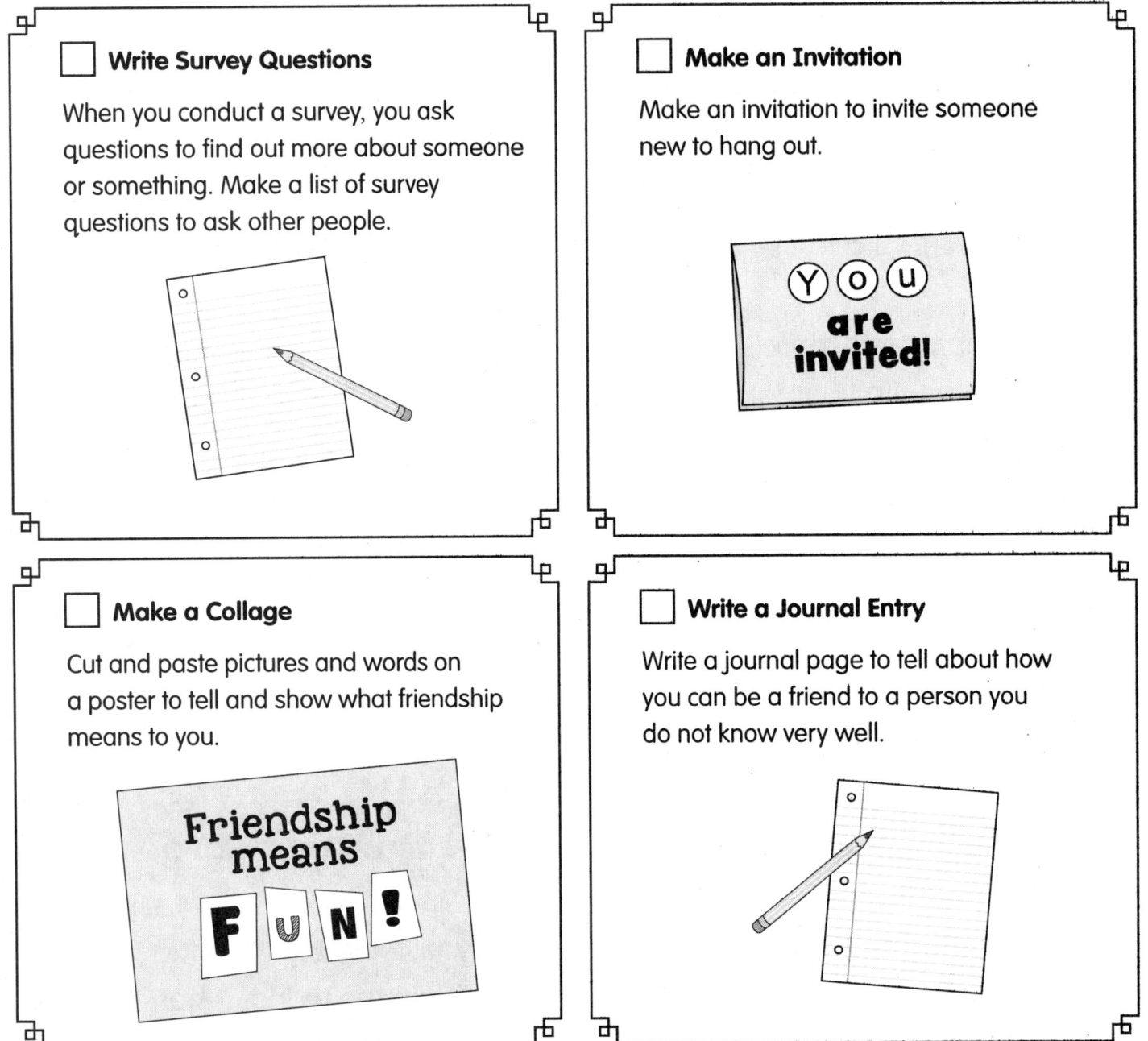

☐ **Write Survey Questions**

When you conduct a survey, you ask questions to find out more about someone or something. Make a list of survey questions to ask other people.

☐ **Make an Invitation**

Make an invitation to invite someone new to hang out.

☐ **Make a Collage**

Cut and paste pictures and words on a poster to tell and show what friendship means to you.

☐ **Write a Journal Entry**

Write a journal page to tell about how you can be a friend to a person you do not know very well.

You Can Be a Friend

Name _____

I Can Be a Friend—Survey Questions

Write survey questions that you could ask to find out more about another person who could be your friend.

What You Need

- a sheet of paper
- a clipboard or a piece of cardboard that is the same size as the paper
- tape
- a pencil

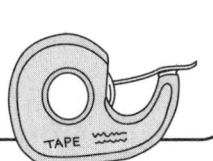

What You Do

1. Think of all the things you can ask someone to find out more about who he or she is. Think about qualities that are important in a friend. Brainstorm your ideas in the box below.
2. Write at least 5 questions on the paper. You can write multiple-choice questions if you want.
3. Attach the survey questions to a clipboard or tape them to a piece of cardboard.
4. Ask a person whom you would like to get to know better the survey questions, and write the person's responses.

Plan Your Survey

You Can Be a Friend

Name _____

I Can Be a Friend—Invitation

Friendships make life more fun and meaningful. Make an invitation to invite someone new to your house.

What You Need

- a sheet of colored construction paper
- a piece of cardboard or poster board
- scissors
- glue or tape
- a pen or marker
- materials to decorate the invitation, such as glitter, dried pasta, cotton balls, colored tissue paper, beads, buttons, foil, etc.

What You Do

1. Cut the construction paper into any shape.
2. Cut the cardboard or poster board into the same shape and size as the construction paper.
3. Write and draw an invitation message on the construction paper. You can invite someone to your house to hang out. You can invite someone to sit next to you on the school bus. Or you can invite someone to do an activity with you.
4. Glue or tape the construction paper onto the cardboard or poster board.
5. Decorate the invitation.
6. Give the invitation to a person whom you want to be friends with.

Plan Your Invitation

You Can Be a Friend   Name _____

I Can Be a Friend—Collage

Make a collage about what friendship means to you. Cut and paste pictures or words to show what you think makes a good friend or what you like to do with your friends.

What You Need

- a sheet of colored construction paper
- scissors
- glue or tape
- magazines or papers with pictures and words that you can cut out
- materials to decorate a collage, such as markers, paint, glitter, cotton balls, foil, colored tissue paper, etc.

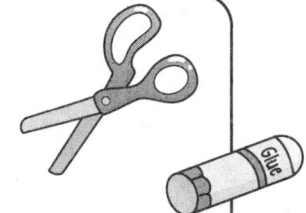

What You Do

1. Cut out pictures or words that show and tell what friendship means to you.
2. You can also write your own words to share your thoughts on what makes a good friend. For example, you can write: "Friends listen to each other."
3. Glue or tape the pictures onto construction paper in any shape or arrangement you want.
4. Use other materials to decorate the construction paper.
5. Hang your collage in your classroom or at home.

Plan Your Collage

You Can Be a Friend Name _____

I Can Be a Friend—Journal Entry

Write a journal entry that helps you think about how to make a new friend.

What You Need

- a sheet of lined paper
- pen or pencil

What You Do

Write your own journal entry. You can use the questions below to help you if needed:

a. How can you invite someone to be your friend?

b. What questions can you ask someone to get to know him or her better?

c. What can you tell the person about yourself?

Plan Your Journal Entry

You Can Accept Changes and Still Be Yourself

Zaina's Diary

This unit is about how we can accept changes in our lives and still be ourselves. Students will read fictional diary entries written by Zaina, a 12-year-old girl who recently immigrated from to the United States from Pakistan. Zaina makes new friends and takes pride in aspects of her original culture while also assimilating to American culture. Students may know people who have immigrated, so they may connect to the story, or they might learn anew how experiencing changes doesn't mean you have to become a different person. As you guide students through these topics, consider their varying world views as they share their experiences and make connections to their own lives.

The pages in this unit are reproducible. Reproduce the unit in its entirety or choose the pages that you wish to have your students do. A suggested teaching path is below.

1. **Read the Realistic Fiction Story (pages 84 and 85)**
   Distribute one copy of the text to each student. Have students read the text independently, or read the text aloud as they follow along silently.

2. **Accepting Changes (page 86)**
   Distribute one copy of the page to each student. Guide students in completing the page independently.

3. **Let's Talk About the Story (page 87)**
   Distribute one copy of the page to each student. Facilitate a whole-group discussion or divide the class into small groups.

   Prepare for discussion:
   Tell students that they will have a conversation with classmates about the questions they have been given. Explain that they do not have to write complete answers to the questions. They can write notes about how they want to answer the questions or how they want to respond to other students' comments. Remind students that they can disagree with or add on to what other students say, as long as all students are respectful.

4. **Talk with Your Partner and Self-Portrait Bookmark (pages 88 and 89)**
   Divide students into groups of two. Distribute one copy of each page to each group. Have each group work on the activity together.

5. **Choose Your Project—Express Yourself (pages 90–94)**
   Distribute one copy of the project menu to each student. Explain to students that they will each choose a project to do. After students have chosen their project, collect the project menus.

   Reproduce and distribute one of the following project pages to each student based on the student's choice: Page 91 for the diary entry; Page 92 for the video diary entry; Page 93 for the sculpture; Page 94 for the song. Decide whether or not students will share their finished projects with the class and instruct students accordingly.

Zaina's Diary

Dear Diary,   March 10

I do not know if this is the right way to start a diary entry. But Ms. Milne told me some people write in a diary to help them deal with big changes in their lives. She said most entries start with "Dear Diary." So that is where I am beginning.

Maybe I should introduce myself? My name is Zaina. My home is in Pakistan. But now I live here in the United States. We have been here six months. My parents say they are happy that we moved to this country. But they do feel worried sometimes. They are worried about finding jobs.

My dad is an engineer. He wants to get a job here, but he cannot work as an engineer until he learns more English. My brother and I began learning English when we were younger in school in Pakistan. My dad and mom are taking an English class together now. They are so excited to practice their English with me and my brother every night. They watch television shows in English. They are learning quickly.

We have a lot of family here, so I have met a lot of cousins, aunts, and uncles whom I never met before. Dad says the U.S. will feel more like home soon. But he also says Pakistan will always be our home. I do not know if this can be true. Can someone call more than one country home?

— Z

Dear Diary,   April 20

It is hard being in a new country. I am most comfortable when I'm around my family. My cousins are from the Pakistani culture, which I am used to. But even when I am with my cousins, I feel a little different. They were born in the U.S. and grew up here. I am new here. I feel like they fit in more. They are older than me and my brother, and they are so nice to us. I love them.

— Z

You Can Accept Changes and Still Be Yourself

Dear Diary, May 4

I have a friend at school. Her name is Virginia, and she is in 6th grade, too. We eat lunch together every day, and I have some classes with her. She asks me questions about where I'm from. She said I have an accent and asked if I speak other languages. I told her that I speak Urdu and a little Pashto. She thought it was so cool, but I don't think it's that special to speak different languages. I have been speaking them since I can remember! LOL. And it's not like I speak Pashto perfectly! I like talking to Virginia a lot. She says things I have never heard before, like "LOL." I went to her house last weekend, and it was so fun. Her mom made us lunch. We had macaroni and cheese and baby carrots. I had never had either of those foods before! Then Virginia came to my house. We listened to music in my room. She asked me where my posters were and said I should hang some posters in my room to show my personality. I want to! I love soccer. Maybe I'll put up some soccer posters!

— Z

Dear Diary, May 25

After school today, I found out that my dad got a job! He is very happy. I knew that he and Mom were worried about finding jobs. I have overheard my parents talking about things that they are worried about. But now I think they feel happier. — Z

Dear Diary, June 4

I decided to try out for the soccer team for next year. My brother plays soccer, and I played soccer in Pakistan. But we didn't call it soccer there. We called it football in Pakistan.

My dad and I talked last night. He said we have had a lot of changes in our lives. He said we can accept these changes and still be ourselves. He is right. I will always be Zaina, a girl from Pakistan and the U.S., a girl who speaks different languages and who loves her family. I will always be Zaina, a girl with a big heart, who has friends and who is loved. — Z

You Can Accept Changes and Still Be Yourself   Name _____

Accepting Changes

Zaina experienced a big change in her life. She moved from Pakistan to the U.S. She felt unsure about this change. But after a while, she began to feel more at home in U.S. Write or draw to tell about 2 times you accepted a big change in your life.

This was a big change in my life…	This feeling started when the change happened…	This is how I accepted the change in my life…

This was a big change in my life…	This feeling started when the change happened…	This is how I accepted the change in my life…

You Can Accept Changes and Still Be Yourself

Name _____

Let's Talk About the Story

Read the questions. Think carefully about how to answer each one. You will talk with classmates about your ideas. There are no wrong answers. Below each question, you can write:

- Things that you want to say  Things other people said that you agree with  Things other people said that you disagree with

1. Zaina immigrated with her family to the U.S. from Pakistan. What do you think it would be like to immigrate to a new country?

2. Do you think someone can be from more than one country? Tell your opinion.

3. Do you think that change means you become a different person? Tell why or why not.

4. Do you think that writing a diary or journal can help you deal with big changes in your life? Why or why not?

© Evan-Moor Corporation • EMC 8266 • Culturally Responsive Lessons and Activities

You Can Accept Changes and Still Be Yourself

Name _____

Name _____

Talk with Your Partner

Changes in our lives can be big or small. Zaina experienced a big change in her life when she immigrated to the U.S. Talk with your partner about big and small changes you have experienced in your lives. Draw or write about those changes in the circles below.

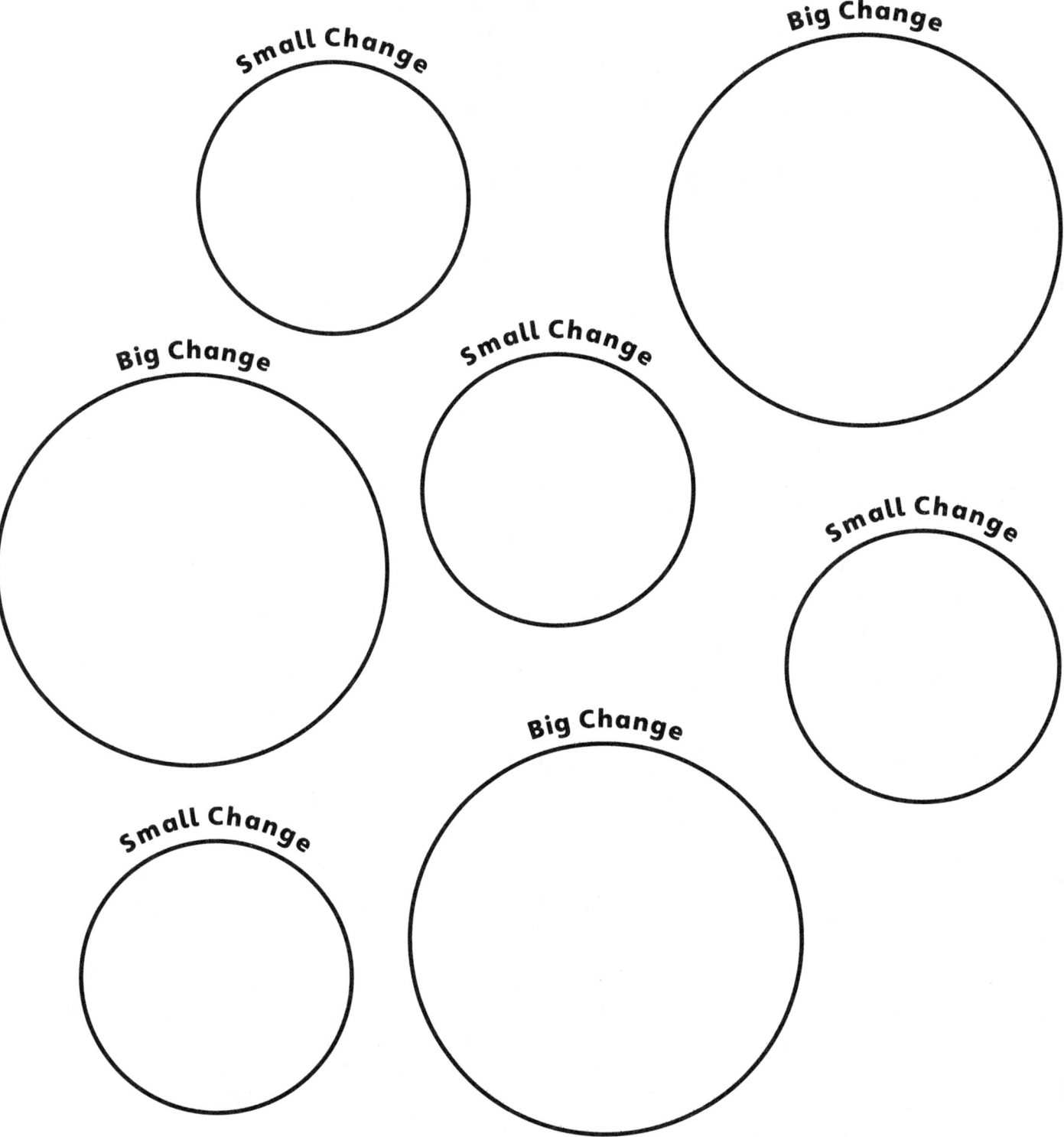

You Can Accept Changes and Still Be Yourself

Self-Portrait Bookmark

You and your partner have both experienced changes in your lives. People can accept changes without losing who they are. Cut out the bookmarks below. Each partner takes one. Draw a self-portrait on the bookmark. Then write things about yourself that you think will never change. Keep your bookmark and use it.

This is who I am!

These things will never change!

_____
_____
_____
_____
_____

This is who I am!

These things will never change!

_____
_____
_____
_____
_____

You Can Accept Changes and Still Be Yourself

Name _____

Choose Your Project—
Express Yourself

Zaina realized that she can accept changes and still be herself. She is a girl from more than one country. She is learning who she is.

1. Think about who you are and big changes you have had in your life. Then choose a project to do from the menu below.

2. Write a ✓ to show which project you choose. Last, give this page to your teacher.

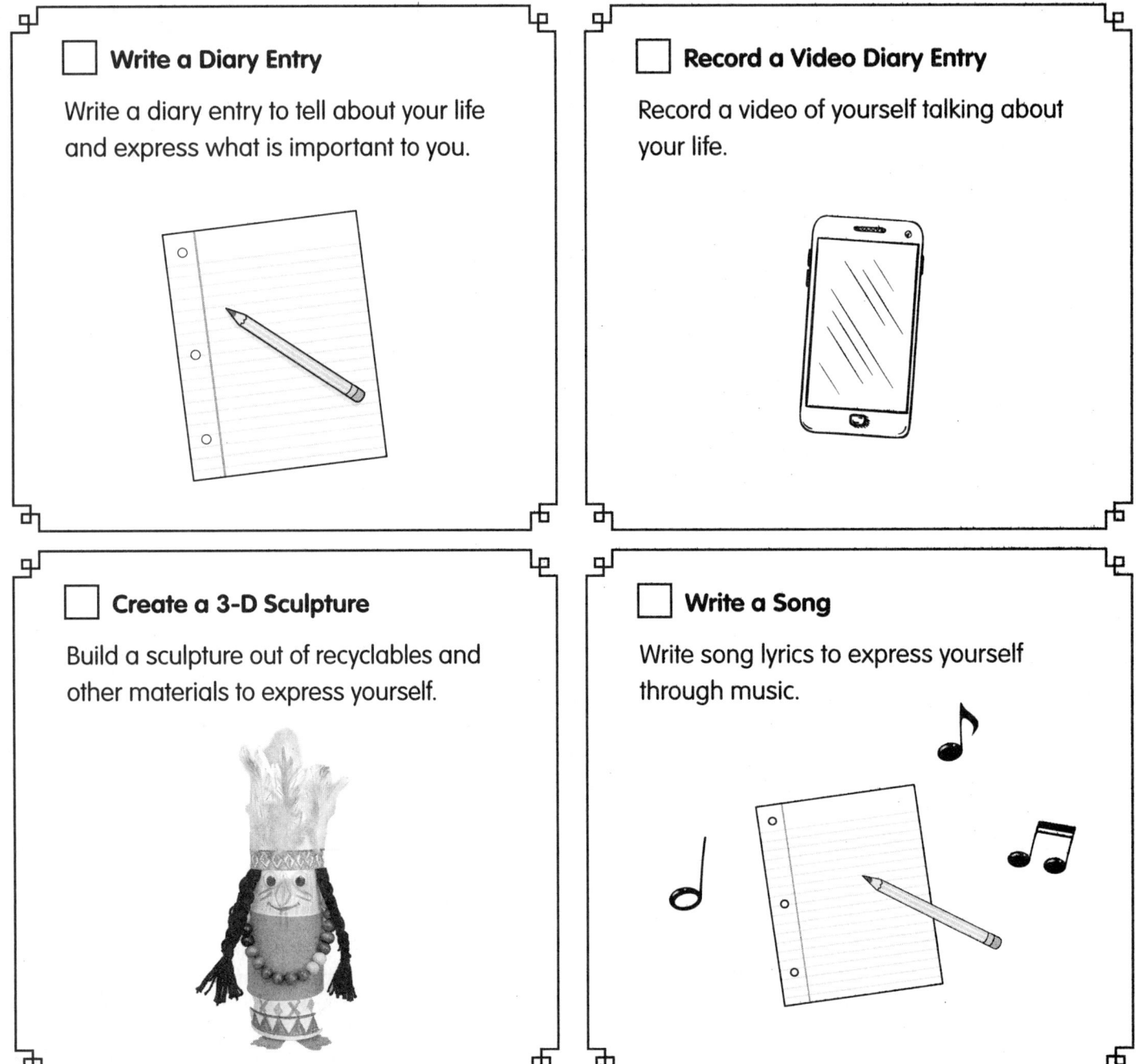

☐ **Write a Diary Entry**

Write a diary entry to tell about your life and express what is important to you.

☐ **Record a Video Diary Entry**

Record a video of yourself talking about your life.

☐ **Create a 3-D Sculpture**

Build a sculpture out of recyclables and other materials to express yourself.

☐ **Write a Song**

Write song lyrics to express yourself through music.

You Can Accept Changes and Still Be Yourself

Name _____

Express Yourself—Diary Entry

Write a diary entry that tells anything you want to talk about.

What You Need

- a sheet of lined paper
- pen or pencil

What You Do

1. Write your diary entry to tell about how your day went or about changes you've had in your life. Use the questions below to help you if needed.

    a. What is something unique or special about you?

    b. What activities do you love to do?

    c. Who are your friends?

    d. What big things have happened in your life?

    e. What is important to you?

2. Save your diary entry. If you liked writing a diary entry, think about getting a diary to write in regularly.

Plan Your Diary Entry

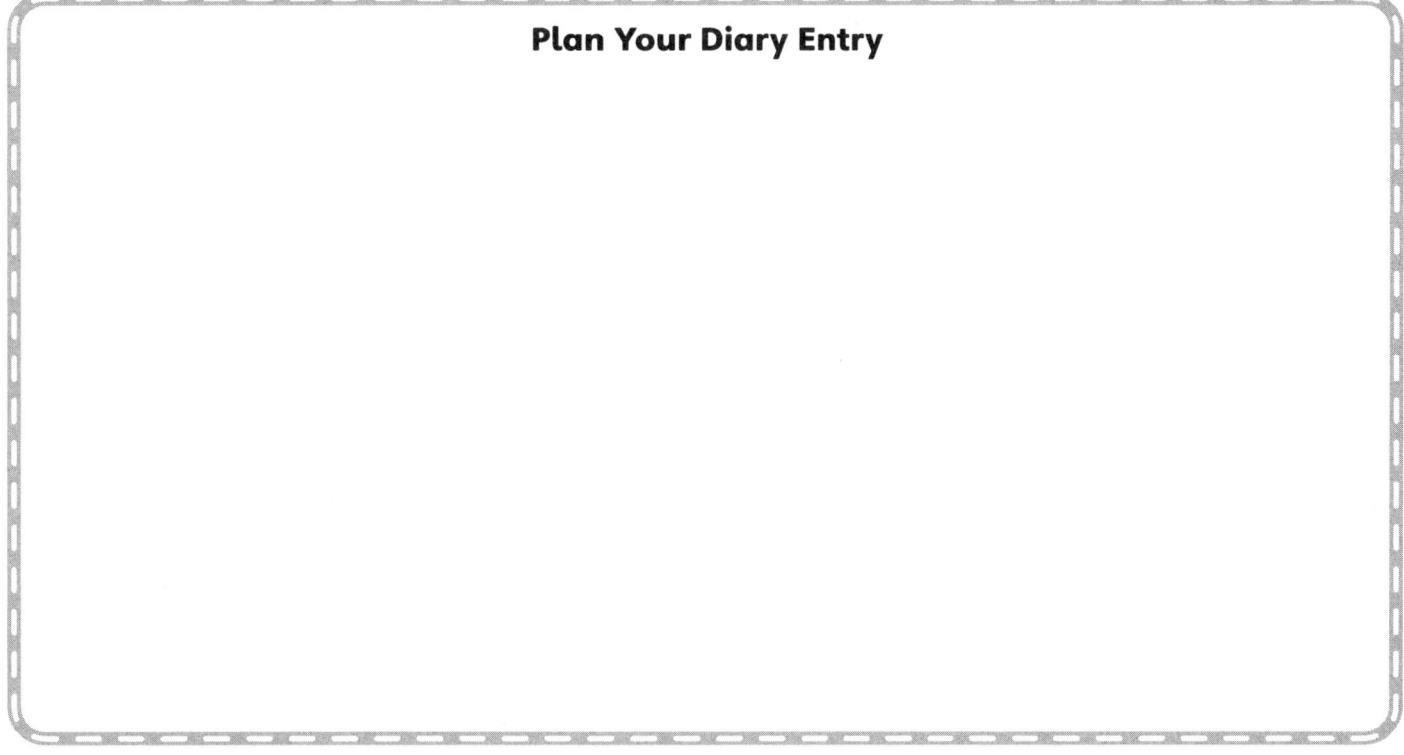

You Can Accept Changes and Still Be Yourself　　Name _____

Express Yourself—Video Diary Entry

Make a video of yourself talking or showing how your day went.

What You Need

- a smartphone or other device for recording

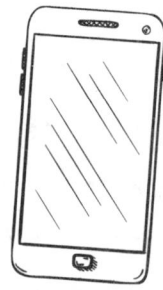

What You Do

1. Record a video diary entry. Say or show whatever you want to tell about yourself or about changes in your life. Use the questions below to help you if needed.

    a. What is something unique or special about you?

    b. What activities do you love to do?

    c. Who are your friends?

    d. What big things have happened in your life?

    e. What is important to you?

2. Save your video diary entry. If you liked making it, consider recording diary entries regularly.

Plan Your Video Diary Entry

You Can Accept Changes and Still Be Yourself

Name _____

Express Yourself—3-D Sculpture

Create a 3-D sculpture out of different materials.

What You Need

- scissors
- glue or tape
- recyclable materials such as tin cans, milk cartons, cardboard boxes or tubes, used tissue paper, empty plastic bottles, etc.
- things to decorate a sculpture such as dried pasta, beads, buttons, cotton balls, paint, glitter, pom-poms, dried leaves, foil, etc.

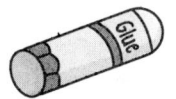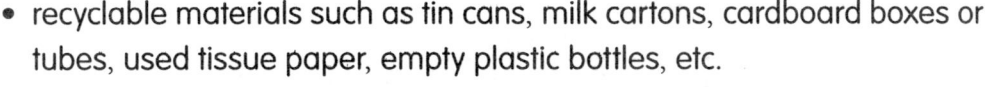

What You Do

1. Pick out some recyclable materials you want to use to make your sculpture. Choose unique or interesting materials that will help you express yourself.
2. Glue or tape your recyclable materials together in any shape or arrangement you want.
3. Use other materials to decorate your sculpture.
4. Display your sculpture in your classroom or at home.

Plan Your Sculpture

You Can Accept Changes and Still Be Yourself

Name _____

Express Yourself—Song

Write song lyrics to express yourself through music.

What You Need
- a song of your choice to imitate
- a pen or pencil
- a smartphone or other device that can record audio

Think of a song with a tune that you would like to sing along to. Write a new title for the song. Then write words to express who you are to the tune of that song. After you finish writing the song, practice singing it. Then record yourself singing your song!

_____
song title

Different Is Good

Celebrating New Experiences

This unit is about celebrating new experiences and realizing that meeting people who have different cultures, customs, and beliefs is a positive thing. The story is about a boy and his mom who recently moved to a new apartment complex and received invitations to parties to celebrate holidays that they are not familiar with. Students may have had similar experiences of being invited to celebrations that they don't know much about, or they may learn through the situations in the story how they can respond to these types of situations. As you guide students through these topics, consider their varying world views as they share their experiences and make connections to their own lives.

The pages in this unit are reproducible. Reproduce the unit in its entirety or choose the pages that you wish to have your students do. A suggested teaching path is below.

1. **Read the Realistic Fiction Story (pages 96 and 97)**
   Distribute one copy of the text to each student. Have students read the text independently, or read the text aloud as they follow along silently.

2. **New and Different (page 98)**
   Distribute one copy of the page to each student. Guide students in completing the page independently.

3. **Let's Talk About the Story (page 99)**
   Distribute one copy of the page to each student. Facilitate a whole-group discussion or divide the class into small groups.

   Prepare for discussion:
   Tell students that they will have a conversation with classmates about the questions they have been given. Explain that they do not have to write complete answers to the questions. They can write notes about how they want to answer the questions or how they want to respond to other students' comments. Remind students that they can disagree with or add on to what other students say, as long as all students are respectful.

4. **Talk with Your Partner and What Would You Say? (pages 100 and 101)**
   Divide students into groups of two. Distribute one copy of each page to each student. Then have each student work on the activity together.

5. **Choose Your Project—Celebrate New and Different (pages 102–106)**
   Distribute one copy of the project menu to each student. Explain to students that they will each choose a project to do. After students have chosen their project, collect the project menus.

   Reproduce and distribute one of the following project pages to each student based on the student's choice: Page 103 for the invitation; Page 104 for the wish list; Page 105 for the video; Page 106 for the party. Decide whether or not students will share their finished projects with the class and instruct students accordingly.

Different Is Good

Celebrating New Experiences

Robert was quiet as he walked down the hall at his family's new apartment complex. His Mom smiled and said hello to everyone they passed. Everyone seemed to have a different nationality. He heard different languages being spoken and smelled foods he did not recognize.

"Mom," whispered Robert. "We are different from everyone else here."

"I know," said his mom. Different is good, Robert. I'm excited to meet everyone at the apartment complex meeting tomorrow. How about you and I decide to celebrate the new experiences we will have living here?" Robert nodded his head in agreement.

Robert and his mom had been in their new apartment for about a month when they started getting invitations to holiday parties.

"Mom, what's a Kwanzaa party?" Robert asked after he ripped open a bright orange envelope and pulled out an invitation with colorful candles and fruits. "The Johnsons invited us to their Kwanzaa party at 1:30 on Sunday, January 1."

"Really? I don't know much about Kwanzaa, but I'd like to get to know the Johnsons better. Why don't you look up Kwanzaa online," said Mom.

"Okay, it says here that Kwanzaa is a week-long celebration that honors African heritage in African American culture," read Robert. "Each day of Kwanzaa is devoted to celebrating the seven values of African culture, which are unity, self-determination, collective work and responsibility, cooperative economics—which means building Black businesses—purpose, creativity, and faith. A candle is lit on each day to celebrate each one of these principles. On the last day, a black candle is lit, and gifts are shared."

"Gosh, Kwanzaa is a really meaningful celebration. I'd like to go to their Kwanzaa party. How about you?" asked Mom.

"Sure!" said Robert. "I'll write it on the calendar for us."

  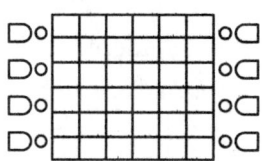  

Different Is Good   Name _____

The next day another invitation was left at their door. Robert opened it up and announced, "Guess what? We got another invitation to a holiday party for this Sunday."

"Really? Who is it from?" asked Mom.

"The Rodríguez family. They are having a Las Posadas celebration this Sunday. I like Manny; he is cool! Can we go?" asked Robert.

"Well, let's find out more about Las Posadas. I have never been to a Las Posadas celebration." replied Mom.

Robert grabbed his tablet and started to read, "Okay, it says here that Las Posadas is an important Mexican Christmas tradition, and many other countries such as Honduras and Spain celebrate it, too. They re-enact the bible story of Mary and Joseph's journey to Bethlehem. They carry candles and sing songs as they walk together to someone's home. Hey! That must be Manny's apartment this time! No wonder it says to bring a candle and meet in the lobby downstairs. It also says that the celebration includes bible readings and a party with piñatas, tamales, and hot drinks."

"Well, we don't really have the same beliefs that Las Posadas celebrates, so I am not sure if we should go, Robert," Mom responded.

"But Mom, you said that different is good and that we should celebrate new experiences. Even though we have different beliefs from the people celebrating Las Posadas, we can go and learn more about it. You never know, Mom, you might like being a part of their celebration."

"You are right, Robert. We can go. I want to honor their holiday traditions and learn more about them," said Mom.

Two more invitations came in by the end of the week. One was for a Hannukah celebration, and the other was for a Christmas party. Robert and his mom went to them with the attitude of being open to celebrating new experiences. Every party was different because of the food, the people, and the meaning behind the celebration. Robert thought about all the new people he had met, the new foods he had tried, and what he had learned about different holiday traditions and customs. "Mom was right," he thought to himself, "different is good."

Different Is Good

Name _____

New and Different

Robert and his mom said "different is good." They liked that they would meet people in their apartment complex who had different cultures, beliefs, and languages.

Do you think that different is good? Fill in the circle of the statement you agree with. Then write two reasons to explain your opinion.

◯ I think that "different is good."   ◯ I do not think that "different is good."

Robert and his mom celebrated new experiences. Write new experiences that you would celebrate.

Different Is Good

Name _____

Let's Talk About the Story

Read the questions. Think carefully about how to answer each one. You will talk with classmates about your ideas. There are no wrong answers. Below each question, you can write:

Things that you want to say

Things other people said that you agree with

Things other people said that you disagree with

1. Do you agree with Robert's mom that you should celebrate new experiences? Why or why not?

2. Robert felt worried when he realized that he and his mom were different from the other people at the apartment complex. Do you understand his feelings? Why or why not?

3. Robert was excited to go to holiday parties that celebrated different beliefs. Would you have wanted to go to those parties? Why or why not?

4. Do you think that it's rude to wish someone a happy holiday if that person does not celebrate that specific holiday? Explain your opinion.

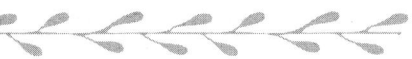

Talk with Your Partner

Complete the chart below to tell what you know about different holiday celebrations and what you'd like to know about each one. Then share what you wrote with your partner. If you learn something new, write it in your chart.

	What I Know	What I Want to Know
Kwanzaa		
Diwali		
Hannukah		
Las Posadas		

Different Is Good

Name _____

What Would You Say?

Read the situations below. Fill in the circle or circles to show what you would tell the kid in the situation. After you finish, compare answers with your partner and tell why you choose those answers.

Andrew's mom wants him to learn something new. She suggested that he learn to play an instrument. He likes playing sports, not playing instruments. Andrew does not want to go to music class. He's thinking about telling his mom that he does not want to learn anything new.

○ Try new things.   ○ Stick to what you know.   ○ Learn a new sport instead.

Krystal went to the hair salon. When she was there, she saw a girl who had purple and pink streaks in her hair. Krystal thought the colorful streaks looked really cool. She asked her mom if she could get them done, too. After her mom said yes, Krystal changed her mind. No one else at school had them, and she did not want to be different.

○ Just be yourself.   ○ Don't stand out.   ○ Just get pink streaks this time.

Jia's school has a cafeteria. They serve sandwiches, pizza, hamburgers, salads, and fruits for lunch. But Jia likes to eat something different for lunch. She likes to eat gimbap, a Korean sushi roll her mom makes. All her friends eat the cafeteria food. She is afraid if she brings gimbap to eat, her friends will think she is weird.

○ Eat what you like.   ○ You should try to fit in.   ○ Offer gimbap to your friends.

© Evan-Moor Corporation • EMC 8266 • Culturally Responsive Lessons and Activities   101

Different Is Good

Name _____

Choose Your Project—
Celebrate New and Different

Robert and his mom went to holiday parties that celebrated beliefs and customs that were new and different to them.

1. Think about celebrations or experiences that are new and different from what you know. Then choose a project to do from the menu below.

2. Write a ✓ to show which project you choose. Last, give this page to your teacher.

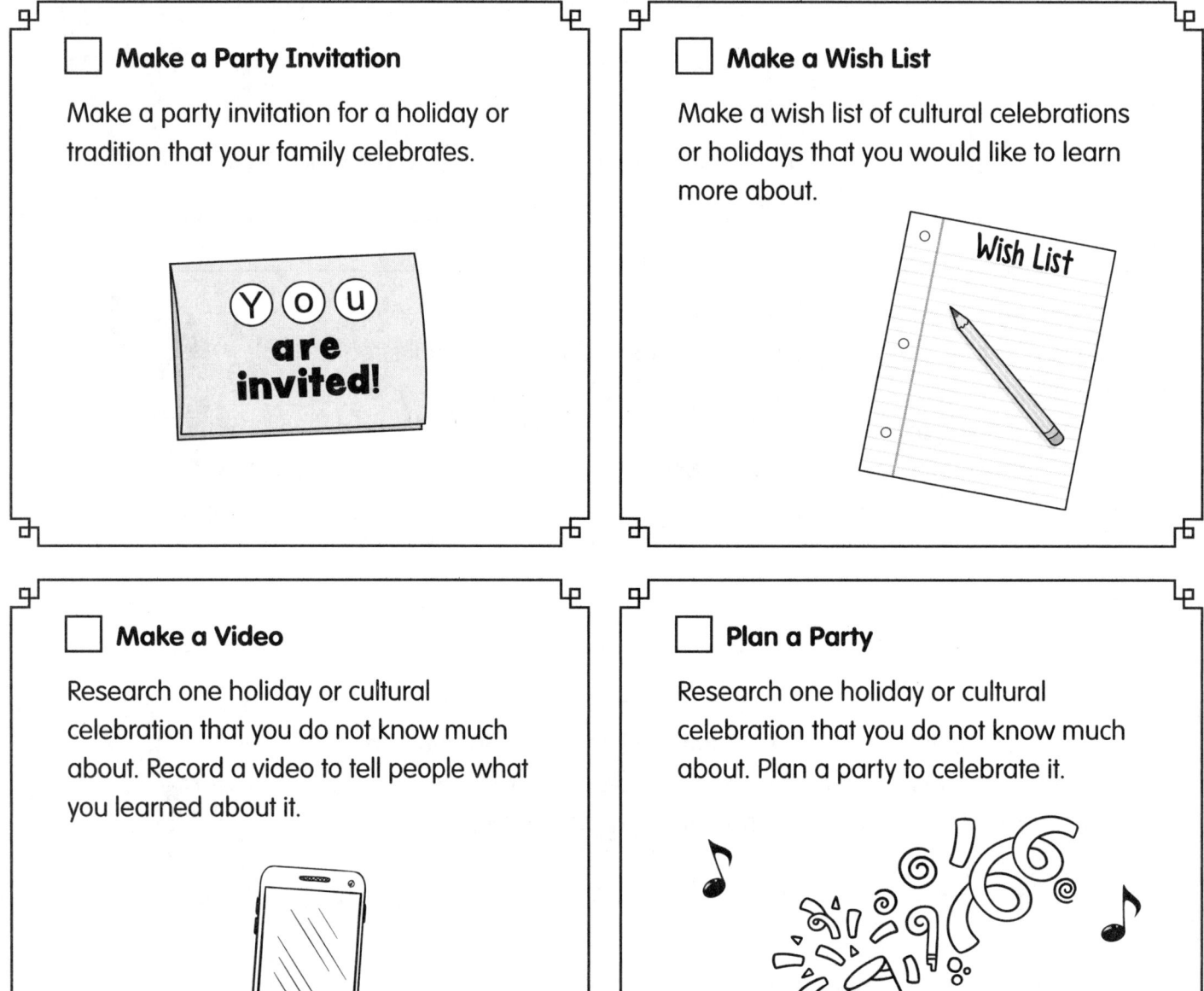

☐ **Make a Party Invitation**

Make a party invitation for a holiday or tradition that your family celebrates.

☐ **Make a Wish List**

Make a wish list of cultural celebrations or holidays that you would like to learn more about.

☐ **Make a Video**

Research one holiday or cultural celebration that you do not know much about. Record a video to tell people what you learned about it.

☐ **Plan a Party**

Research one holiday or cultural celebration that you do not know much about. Plan a party to celebrate it.

Different Is Good Name _____

Celebrate New and Different—Invitation

Make a party invitation for a holiday or cultural tradition that you and your family celebrate. Include information about why the holiday or celebration is meaningful to you.

What You Need

- a sheet of construction paper
- colored pencils or markers
- a pen
- glue
- scissors
- materials to decorate the invitation, such as felt, stickers, glitter, colored tissue paper, etc.

What You Do

1. Choose a holiday or tradition to make a party invitation for.
2. Think about why the holiday or tradition is meaningful to you and write about it below.
3. Fold the construction paper in half as shown above to make an invitation.
4. Write a message on the front of the invitation and decorate it.
5. On the inside, write the date, time, and place for the party. Explain what you will do at the party and write why the celebration is meaningful to you.
6. Show your invitation to someone.

This is why this celebration is meaningful to me:

Different Is Good

Name _____

Celebrate New and Different—Wish List

Make a wish list of holidays or cultural traditions that you would like to learn more about. Put a star next to ones that you would like to attend a celebration for.

What You Need

- a sheet of paper
- colored pencils
- a device to do online research

What You Do

1. Do online research about holidays and cultural traditions. These are some suggestions for search terms:

    "Cultural celebrations"   "Traditions in Kenya"   "Holidays"

2. Choose the holidays and cultural celebrations you want to put on your wish list to learn more about.

3. Put a star next to the holidays and cultural traditions that you would like to attend a celebration for.

4. Show your wish list to your family and tell them what you know about the holidays and cultural traditions.

Plan Your Wish List

Different Is Good

Name _____

Celebrate New and Different—Video

Research holidays and celebrations that you do not know much about. Choose the one you are most interested in and record a video to tell people what you learned about it.

What You Need

- a smartphone or other device to record a video
- a device to do online research

Optional: supplies to decorate a space to record your video

What You Do

1. Do online research about holidays and cultural traditions. These are some suggestions for search terms:

    "Cultural celebrations"   "Traditions in Kenya"   "Holidays"

2. Choose one that you want to do more research about. Read about the holiday or tradition and look at pictures that are posted online that show you more details about the holiday or celebration, such as symbols.

3. Use the outline below or make your own to plan what you will talk about in your video.

4. Record your video and show it to your family and friends.

Video Planning Outline

The name of the holiday or tradition

Who celebrates it

Why you chose it

What you want to tell people about it

© Evan-Moor Corporation • EMC 8266 • Culturally Responsive Lessons and Activities   **105**

Different Is Good Name _____

Celebrate New and Different—Party

Choose a holiday or cultural tradition that you don't know a lot about, do research to learn more about it, and plan a party to celebrate it!

What You Need

- a device to do online research
- paper and pen or a computer to plan the party

What You Do

1. Research the holiday or cultural tradition. Write notes about what you learn. Look at pictures and images that show the celebration.
2. Use the outline below or make your own to plan your party.
3. If you want to, a month before the special holiday or celebration takes place, ask your parents if this party is something you can do with their help.

Party Planning Outline

What we are celebrating

When this holiday or tradition takes place on the calendar

Traditions or customs we will follow

Colors and symbols I will use to decorate

Songs we will listen to

Games we will play

Food we will eat

People I will invite

Let's Celebrate Who We Are

This unit is about your students. The goal of this unit is to foster a sense of belonging for every student. Every student deserves to feel safe and proud when sharing about his or her own culture and life. When we talk about culture in this unit, we are not only referring to students' ethnic or national cultures, but also their social cultures, which includes students' values, stories, traditions, interests, struggles, and more. One way to help all students feel a sense of belonging is for them to share about themselves and learn about each other.

The pages in this unit are reproducible. Reproduce the unit in its entirety or choose the pages that you wish to have your students do.

1. **Let's Talk About Culture (page 108)**
   Distribute one copy of the page to each student. Facilitate a whole-group discussion or divide the class into small groups. Explain to students that they do not have to write complete answers to the questions. They can write notes about what they would like to say during the discussion.

2. **Heads Down, Palms Up! (pages 109 and 110)**
   Distribute one copy of the activity page and one copy of the fact cards on page 110 to each student. Provide students with the other materials needed for this activity and facilitate the game.

3. **This Makes Me Happy (page 111)**
   Distribute one copy of the page to each student. Provide the materials needed for the activity.

4. **Same and Different Handprints (page 112)**
   Distribute one copy of the page to each student. Provide the materials needed for the activity. Plan the space where you will display the handprints for students to compare.

5. **Give Shout-outs! (pages 113 and 114)**
   Distribute one copy of each page to each student. Provide the materials needed for the activity.

6. **Questions for Parent/Guardian and A Bit About Me, A Bit About You (pages 115 and 116)**
   Distribute one copy of page 115 to each student. This page is for students to take home. After students return the page to you, use the answers to form questions to ask each student during the circle discussion for A Bit About Me, A Bit About You. Before beginning the discussion, distribute the appropriate number of copies of page 116 to each student.

7. **Do You Agree? (pages 117 and 118)**
   Reproduce multiple copies of the sentences on page 118 as needed and cut them out. Then distribute one copy of the activity on page 117 and one sentence to each student. Provide the other materials needed for the activity.

Let's Celebrate Who We Are

Name _____

Let's Talk About Culture

Read the questions. Think carefully about how to answer each one.
You will talk with classmates about your ideas. There are no wrong answers.
Below each question, you can write:

| Things that you want to say | | Things other people said that you agree with | | Things other people said that you disagree with |

1. Every person is different from other people, but all people are the same in many ways, too. Do you think it is good or not good that every person is so different from everyone else?

2. Do you believe that all people can choose to be kind or mean? Tell what you believe and why.

3. What are some of the ways that all people are the same, no matter where they live or what they look like?

4. What are some of the things that make you and your family different from other families?

Let's Celebrate Who We Are

Name _____

Heads Down, Palms Up!

Play a fun game to learn about your classmates.

What You Need

- clear desktop or tabletop space and chair for each player
- fact cards on page 110
- a pencil or pen
- scissors
- a small baggie for each player

What You Do

1. Write a fact about yourself on each card on page 110. Then cut out the cards and put them into the baggie without showing anybody what you wrote. Keep the baggie with you.

2. The teacher will choose 5 players to stand at the front of the classroom. All other players must close their eyes, put their head down on the desktop or tabletop, and stretch one hand out with the palm facing up.

3. Each of the 5 standing players will take one of the fact cards he or she wrote and place it in the palm of a sitting player. Then the 5 players return to their places at the front of the room. The sitting players must keep their eyes closed until the teacher instructs them to sit up and open their eyes.

4. When the sitting players open their eyes, those with a card read it and stand up. Then they each get one turn to try to guess whose card it is. If a player guesses correctly, he or she trades places with that person. If a player does not guess correctly, the player sits down.

5. Players should throw away the fact cards already used in the game. Then repeat steps 2 through 4 to play another round of the game.

6. For each round, standing players should place fact cards in the palms of players who have not yet had a turn in the game. Do this until all players have either had a turn to stand or receive a card.

© Evan-Moor Corporation • EMC 8266 • Culturally Responsive Lessons and Activities

Let's Celebrate Who We Are

Fact: _____
_____
_____

Fact: _____
_____
_____

Fact: _____
_____
_____

Fact: _____
_____
_____

Fact: _____
_____
_____

Fact: _____
_____
_____

Fact: _____
_____
_____

Fact: _____
_____
_____

Fact: _____
_____
_____

Fact: _____
_____
_____

Let's Celebrate Who We Are

Name _____

This Makes Me Happy

Make a poster that shows things that make you happy.

What You Need

- large poster board
- pictures of objects, people, food, animals, activities, and places that make you happy, or anything else that makes you happy
- markers
- scissors
- glue or tape
- materials to decorate the poster, such as glitter, dried cereal, colored tissue paper, stamps, foil, paint, yarn, beads, buttons, etc.

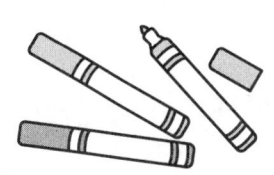

What You Do

1. Write the words **This Makes Me Happy** at the top of the poster. Then write your name somewhere on the poster.
2. Draw and tape or glue pictures onto the poster. Next to each picture, write to tell what the picture shows and why it makes you happy.
3. Decorate the poster.
4. Show your poster to your class or hang it up somewhere you will see it often to remind you of all the things that make you so happy!

Let's Celebrate Who We Are

Name _____

Same and Different Handprints

All people have differences and similarities. We all look kind of the same and kind of different. Compare your handprints with your classmates' handprints to see one way you are all the same and different.

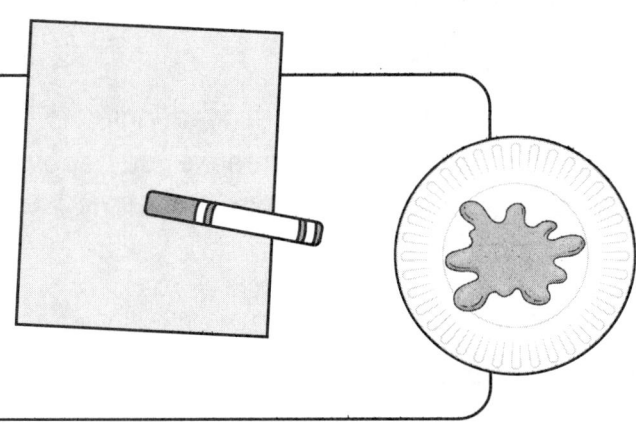

What You Need

- paint
- light-colored construction paper
- marker
- paper plate
- a place to hang or lay out all of the handprints

What You Do

1. Use the marker to write your name on the construction paper.
2. Pour paint onto the paper plate.
3. Dip each hand into the paint. Then press your hands onto the construction paper.
4. Let the paint dry. Then put your handprints with your classmates'.
5. Look at all of the handprints with your classmates and talk about how they are the same. Also talk about any differences you see.

Let's Celebrate Who We Are   Name _____

Give Shout-outs!

A shout-out is something you say to tell someone thanks or that they did a good job. Give shout-outs to the people in your family, and share the shout-outs with your class!

What You Need

- page 114
- colored construction paper
- scissors
- tape or glue
- crayons or markers

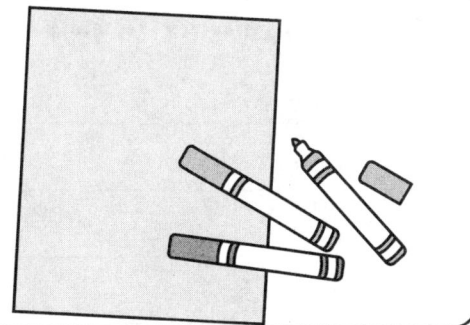

What You Do

1. Think of someone in your family whom you want to give a shout-out to.
2. Write inside each star on page 114 to tell whom each shout-out is for, and write what that person did to help you or make you happy. Or you can write something that the person did well.
3. Color the stars.
4. Cut out each star. Then tape or glue each one onto the construction paper.
5. Cut out each star again, leaving a border of the construction paper.
6. Share the shout-outs you made with your class. Tell the class why you are giving those people a shout-out.
7. Take your shout-outs home or give each one to the person you made it for.

Let's Celebrate Who We Are

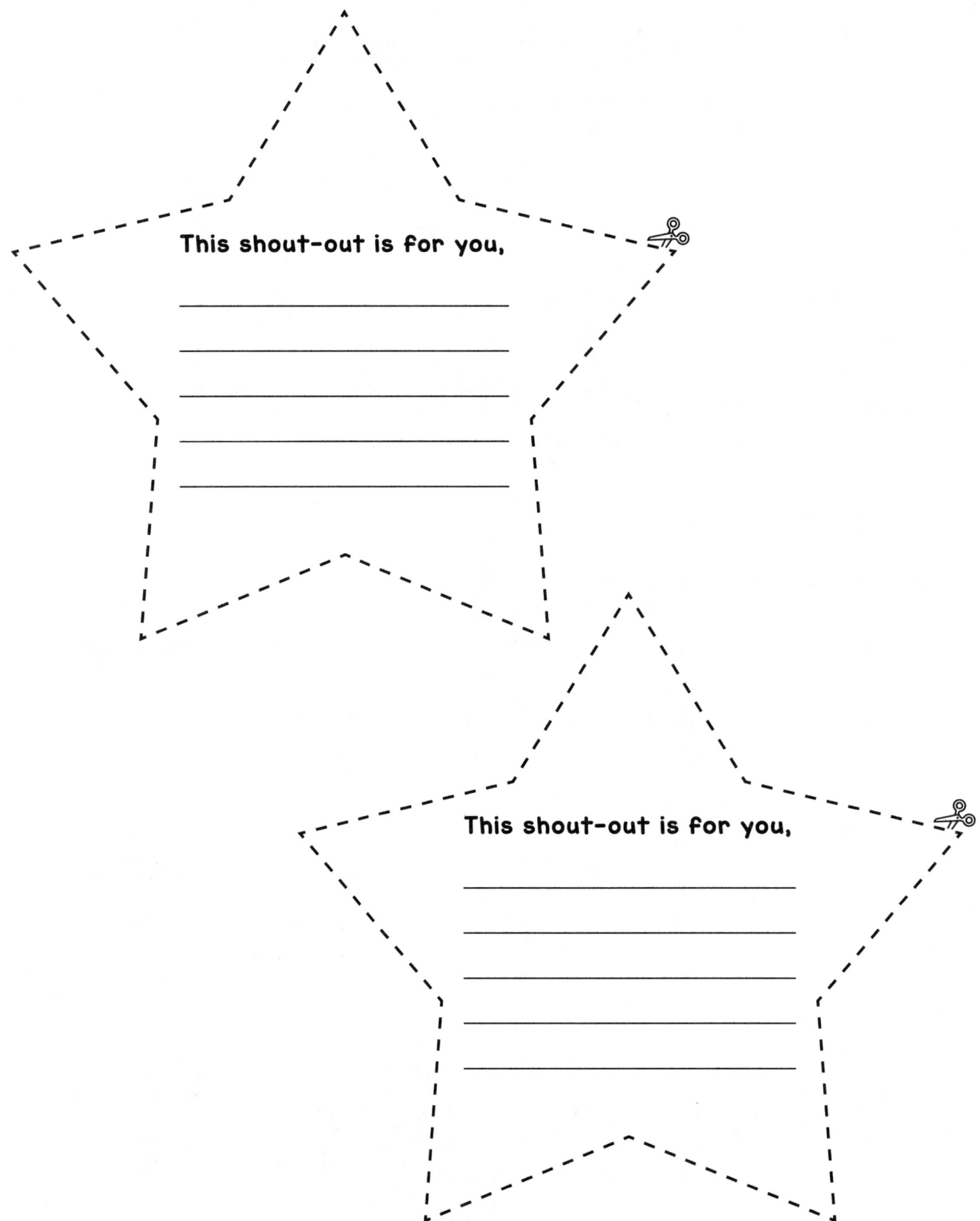

Let's Celebrate Who We Are   Name _____

Questions for Parent/Guardian

Every group of people has its own culture. Different families have their own cultures. Your culture includes the things you like to do, the foods you eat, the music you listen to, and much more! Take this page home, and ask an adult to write answers to the questions. Then bring this page back to your teacher.

1. What are some family traditions or activities that your family does together? Or are there any interests or hobbies that all of your family members enjoy?

   _____
   _____
   _____

2. What is something your child is proud of himself or herself about and likes to talk about?

   _____
   _____
   _____

3. Is there anything you have done as a family that is cultural in relation to ethnicity or nationality? Or are there any special events, holidays, or vacations you have done together as a family?

   _____
   _____
   _____

4. Is there anything else your child likes to talk about, such as an interest, an experience, or a fact about your family?

   _____
   _____
   _____

5. Are there any special foods or events your child looks forward to every week or every year?

   _____
   _____
   _____

Let's Celebrate Who We Are

Name _____

A Bit About Me, A Bit About You

Sit in a circle with your classmates. Write the names of all of your classmates. The teacher will ask each student questions. When it is your turn to answer questions, only you can talk. When it is another student's turn, listen carefully and then write one thing you learned about that person next to his or her name.

Name	What I learned about this person

Let's Celebrate Who We Are   Name _____

Do You Agree?

Every person has his or her own opinions and beliefs. Sometimes we share beliefs with other people and sometimes we don't, and that is okay. Do this activity to tell what some of your beliefs are.

What You Need

- blown-up balloon
- markers
- a sentence that the teacher provides
- an area of the room to put all of the blown-up balloons where all students can reach them

What You Do

1. Read the sentence that the teacher gives you. Then use a marker to write this sentence on your balloon.

2. If you agree with the sentence, write your name on the balloon. If you do NOT agree with the sentence, do not write your name.

3. Put your balloon in the area where all students are putting their balloons. The balloons will stay in this area.

4. Try to read as many balloons as you can. Read the sentences and read the students' names to see who agreed and who did not. Write your name on each balloon that you agree with.

5. When all students have finished reading and signing the balloons, talk with your classmates about the sentences you agreed with and the ones you didn't agree with.

Let's Celebrate Who We Are

Balloon Statements

All people deserve to be treated with kindness and respect.	I can be friends with someone even if they have very different opinions from mine.
I feel more comfortable with people who look kind of like me, and I feel uncomfortable around people who look different.	I dislike people who have a different opinion from mine.
No matter what a person looks like, all people should be treated fairly.	I would rather have lots of gifts and things instead of friends.
I would like to have friends who look different from each other and who speak different languages.	I think all countries are just as good as each other.
I wish that nobody in the world would ever get hurt ever again.	Some people deserve to be treated badly.
You can tell how someone will act just by looking at that person.	All people deserve friends.
I love all people, no matter where they are from or what they look like.	Kindness and fairness are very important to me.

Food Is Part of Culture

This unit is about food and how it is an important part of every person's life experience. People need food to live. Yet we do not use food for survival only. We socialize with other people while we eat food. Many people eat certain foods only with their families. For some people it is a joy to eat daily meals with their loved ones. And food can be meaningful. Some people eat specific foods on specific occasions. Some people make or give food to others to show love. Some people like making foods with their friends and families. Food can help us remember times from the past and traditions. Every person's food preferences are different, but they are influenced by our cultures and our lives. Some people like trying many different kinds of foods, and some people do not. Keep in mind that food insecurity may be a very real problem for some of your students. Also, access to different kinds of foods differs for people based on geographic location and other factors. As you guide students through these topics, consider their varying world views as they share their experiences and make connections to their own lives.

The pages in this unit are reproducible. Reproduce the unit in its entirety or choose the pages that you wish to have your students do.

1. **Use Your Noodle! (pages 120 and 121)**
   Distribute one copy of each page to each student. Guide students in completing the pages independently.

2. **Have You Tried This Fruity Fruit? (pages 122 and 123)**
   Distribute one copy of each page to each student. Guide students in completing the pages independently. Then have students share their answers.

3. **Game Day Foods (page 124)**
   Distribute one copy of the page to each student. Guide students in completing the page independently. Then have students share their answers.

4. **New Year Celebration Foods (page 125)**
   Distribute one copy of the page to each student. Guide students in completing the page independently. Then have students share their answers.

5. **Make Your Perfect Celebration Plate (pages 126–128)**
   Distribute one copy of each page to each student. Guide students in completing the pages independently. Then have students share their answers.

6. **Twenty Questions Food Game (pages 129 and 130)**
   Distribute one copy of each page to each student. Provide students with the materials needed. Guide students in making and playing the game.

Food Is Part of Culture

Name _____

Use Your Noodle!

Many people in different countries like to eat noodles. There are so many different ways to eat noodles! Look at the pictures and read about the noodles below and on page 121. Color the circle under the kinds you have tried.

Italy – Ravioli

Pasta pockets filled with meat, cheese, or vegetables

○

Japan – Udon

Thick, chewy noodles that are often eaten in soup or with meat and vegetables

○

Fast Fact:

The country named for each noodle is not the only country where this food is eaten.

Argentina – Ñoquis

Dumplings (small lumps of dough), also known as gnocchi, which can be covered in sauce

○

Austria – Spaetzle

Small dumplings made with fresh eggs and often served with meat or gravy

○

Philippines – Pancit

Thin, long noodles cooked with spices, vegetables, and meat

○

Use Your Noodle!, continued

Afghanistan – Ashak
Pasta dumplings filled with green onions and topped with tomato, mint, garlic, and plain yogurt

○

Egypt – Koshary
Macaroni mixed with lentils, rice, tomatoes, onion, spices, oil, and vinegar

○

Greece – Orzo
Short-cut pasta that looks like rice

○

Morocco – Couscous
Tiny rolled-up balls of pasta that are so small they look like grain

○

Thailand – Pad Thai
Thick, flat rice noodles that are cooked with spices, onions, and often meat, seafood, tofu, or vegetables

○

China – Cellophane Noodles
Long noodles that are so clear they are also known as glass noodles, used in hot soups and stir-fries

○

Food Is Part of Culture

Name _____

Have You Tried This Fruity Fruit?

In some places, some fruits don't grow or can't be found easily. For example, some people eat pineapples almost every day because there are so many where they live. But some people have never even tried a pineapple!

Look at the photos and read the names of the fruits. Then fill in **yes** or **no** to tell if you have tried it before, or fill in **I would try it**.

coconut
- ○ yes
- ○ no
- ○ I would try it

watermelon
- ○ yes
- ○ no
- ○ I would try it

pomegranate
- ○ yes
- ○ no
- ○ I would try it

papaya
- ○ yes
- ○ no
- ○ I would try it

dragon fruit
- ○ yes
- ○ no
- ○ I would try it

persimmon
- ○ yes
- ○ no
- ○ I would try it

blueberry
- ○ yes
- ○ no
- ○ I would try it

cherry
- ○ yes
- ○ no
- ○ I would try it

nectarine
- ○ yes
- ○ no
- ○ I would try it

Food Is Part of Culture

Name _____

Have You Tried This Fruity Fruit?, *continued*

custard apple

- ○ yes
- ○ no
- ○ I would try it

mango

- ○ yes
- ○ no
- ○ I would try it

passion fruit

- ○ yes
- ○ no
- ○ I would try it

breadfruit

- ○ yes
- ○ no
- ○ I would try it

raspberry

- ○ yes
- ○ no
- ○ I would try it

guava

- ○ yes
- ○ no
- ○ I would try it

kiwi

- ○ yes
- ○ no
- ○ I would try it

plum

- ○ yes
- ○ no
- ○ I would try it

star fruit

- ○ yes
- ○ no
- ○ I would try it

© Evan-Moor Corporation • EMC 8266 • Culturally Responsive Lessons and Activities

Food Is Part of Culture Name _____

Game Day Foods

It's the day of the big rugby game. It's showing on TV around the world. Many families are watching the game together, and each family has its own favorite foods for game days. Read what each family eats and look at the photos. Color the face to show if you would want to eat those foods.

The Park family is watching the game from South Korea.
These are their favorite game day snacks:

crunchy dried squid   rice cakes in sauce   potato chips

The Farooqi family is from Pakistan, but they are in Britain watching the game.
These are their favorite game day snacks:

spiced chickpeas   meat pies   chips, or fries

The Garcia family is Mexican American. They are watching the game from the U.S.
These are their favorite game day snacks:

hot dogs   elote, or corn with toppings   chicken wings

Food Is Part of Culture

Name _____

New Year Celebration Foods

Many different cultures celebrate the start of a new year. Different cultures or countries celebrate new year holidays at different times. For example, people in many countries celebrate New Year's Day on January 1 of each year. Many people in Iran and around the world celebrate Nowruz, the Iranian New Year, in March. People in many countries celebrate the Lunar New Year in February. Some people choose to celebrate the new year with special foods.

Look at the photos and read the sentences about the foods that each family makes to celebrate. Write a ✓ in the box to tell if you would want to eat what that family eats.

The Williams family makes a big seafood dinner.

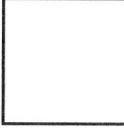

The Lopez family always puts out a spread of different kinds of cheeses to enjoy for the new year.

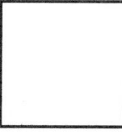

The Gupta family makes a huge pot of spicy stew to share.

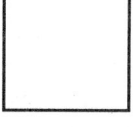

The Ryan family always makes homemade fried chicken and biscuits for the new year.

© Evan-Moor Corporation • EMC 8266 • Culturally Responsive Lessons and Activities

Food Is Part of Culture

Make Your Perfect Celebration Plate

Look at the photos below and on page 127. They show some foods that you may choose to eat for a special celebration. Cut out the foods that you would want to eat or try for the first time, and glue them onto the plate on page 128. On the lines, write why you chose each food. Last, compare your plate to your friends' plates!

Food Is Part of Culture

Food Is Part of Culture Name _____

This is why I chose these foods:

_____
_____
_____
_____

Food Is Part of Culture

Name _____

Twenty Questions Food Game

Make a game about food that you can play with your friends and family. You can play with 2 or more people.

What You Need

- page 130
- scissors

What You Do

1. Cut out the cards on page 130.
2. Look at the photos on the cards and read about the foods. Keep in mind that each food is eaten in more than one country and not only the countries listed on the cards.

To Play

1. Place the cards facedown in a pile. Put the Master Foods List card where every player can see it.
2. When it is each person's turn, that person picks the top card and does not show it to anybody else.
3. The other player or players can ask 20 questions to try to guess what food the person has on his or her card. All of the questions must be yes-or-no questions.

Have Fun!

Food Is Part of Culture

Master Foods List

Peri Peri Chicken	Poutine	Pho
Frikadeller	Paella	Moussaka
Amok Trey		

Peri Peri Chicken
South Africa, Portugal

Chicken cooked in a blend of spices, chiles, and flavors

Poutine   Canada

Potato fries topped with gravy and cheese curds

Pho   Vietnam

Soup filled with rice noodles and meat or vegetables, usually served with lime and mung bean sprouts

Frikadeller   Denmark

Mashed meat patties made of minced beef, milk, onions, and eggs

Paella   Spain

Rice cooked in a broth with tomatoes and vegetables or meat, sometimes spicy

Moussaka   Greece

Layers of eggplant and a cheesy sauce, sometimes also with potatoes or meat

Amok Trey   Cambodia

Fish coated in coconut milk and served in a banana leaf with vegetables

Class Book

This unit provides resources for you and your students to make a Class Book. The purpose of the book is for students to learn more about themselves and each other. It also helps you learn more about each of your students. As you introduce this project to students, keep in mind that some students may be happy to share details about themselves, and others may not feel comfortable doing so. It is important to create a safe space for students to share without feeling judged or uncomfortable about who they are and where they come from. This is intended to be an inclusive experience that creates positive relationships and fosters understanding of each other.

Getting Started

Reproduce the student pages for each student and allow them to complete the pages they wish to. Provide colored pencils, crayons, markers, decorative materials, scissors, and tape and glue for students. Each page students complete will be taped onto a sheet of colored construction paper.

1. **Our Class Book (page 133)**
   Distribute one copy of the page to each student. Have students read the text independently, or read the text aloud as they follow along silently.

2. **About Me (pages 134–136)**
   Distribute one copy of each page to each student. These questions are intended to guide students to reflect on themselves. Provide a quiet space for students to complete this activity. You may also wish to have them work on it at home. Explain that they can complete whatever items they wish to. Encourage students to make their pages colorful and unique by coloring and decorating them. Have them turn in their completed pages to you.

3. **My Family's Culture (pages 137–139)**
   Distribute one copy of each page to each student. Explain that not all of the activities may apply to every student, so they can choose to complete the activities that do apply. Encourage students to take these activities home to complete so they can share them with their families and get information from family members. Have students turn in their completed pages to you.

4. **My Name Page (pages 140–142)**
   Students will make a name page to start their section of the Class Book. There are three pages of alphabet letters. You may wish to provide many copies and have students share and use what they need. Students will color the letters of their name, cut them out, and glue them onto the sheet of construction paper you provide. Then they will write any special information they have about their name. Explain this part of the activity to students by asking them what they know about their name. Were they named after someone in their family? Does their name have a special meaning? If they do not know, encourage them to ask their family about it. Tell students to include any special information about their name on their name page. Have them turn in their completed pages to you.

5. **My Photo or Picture (page 143)**

   Distribute one copy of the page to each student. Explain to students that it is optional to include pictures of themselves in the class book. You may choose to take photographs of your students in the classroom and print them at school.

6. **My Dedication Page (page 144)**

   Distribute one copy of the page to each student. Explain to students that writing a dedication is optional.

7. **Creating the Class Book**

   What You Need

   - 1 sheet of construction paper for each activity page students complete
   - 2 pieces of poster board for the front and back covers
   - 3 loose leaf binder rings to hold the book together
   - 3-hole punch
   - tape

   What You Do

   - Give students the pages that they completed along with the corresponding number of sheets of construction paper. Have students tape each of their pages onto a sheet of construction paper and return them to you. Their My Name Page will already be on construction paper.
   - Gather all students' pages and either three-hole punch the pages yourself or have the students do it. Then use binder rings to assemble the pages into a book. Each student's name page will start that student's section of the book.
   - Use the poster board to create a front and a back cover for the book.

8. **Sharing the Class Book**

   There are many ways to approach sharing the Class Book. You know what will work best for your class. You may wish to consider the suggestions below:

   - Create a sign-up sheet for students to sign out the Class Book. Set aside a special time in class for that student to read the book. Give each student three days to look at it.
   - Allow each student to look at the book on a rotating schedule during reading time.
   - Draw craft sticks each week to see who gets to look at the book for the week. If the student finishes early, you can draw another craft stick and allow the next student to start their turn with the book.

Class Book   Name _____

Our Class Book

Have you ever heard of a Class Book? It is a book that tells each person's story. Read the questions and answers about a Class Book.

Why is a Class Book important?

There are many students in your class. Some of them are your friends, and others you may not know as well. Think about if you walk into a room full of friends. How do you feel? Think about if you walk into a room full of people you don't know. How do you feel? Each person may feel differently.

When you make a Class Book, you get to know the people you are around every day. You learn things about them that you may have never known. You may understand them more. And when you understand them more, you may even become friends. A Class Book also helps your teacher get to know you better. You can show and tell things about yourself that you are proud of or that make you feel happy. You can also show and tell about things that are hard for you or that make you feel sad. When your teacher knows more about you, he or she can give you support when you need it.

How does a Class Book work?

Each student in your class completes pages for the book. You can complete the pages in any way you'd like to. You can be creative and show who you are through drawing pictures or writing. Some of the pages have activities that you complete with your family. After you finish the pages, you give them to your teacher. Then you and your classmates will work together in class to put together the Class Book. The book will be passed around and each student will have his or her own time to look through it. You will learn a lot about everyone and have a lot of fun reading the book!

© Evan-Moor Corporation • EMC 8266 • Culturally Responsive Lessons and Activities

Class Book   Name _____

About Me

Draw and write to tell about you.

What I like to do most:

5 things that are important to me are:

I am a star at:

Class Book

Name _____

About Me, *continued*

Draw and write to tell about you.

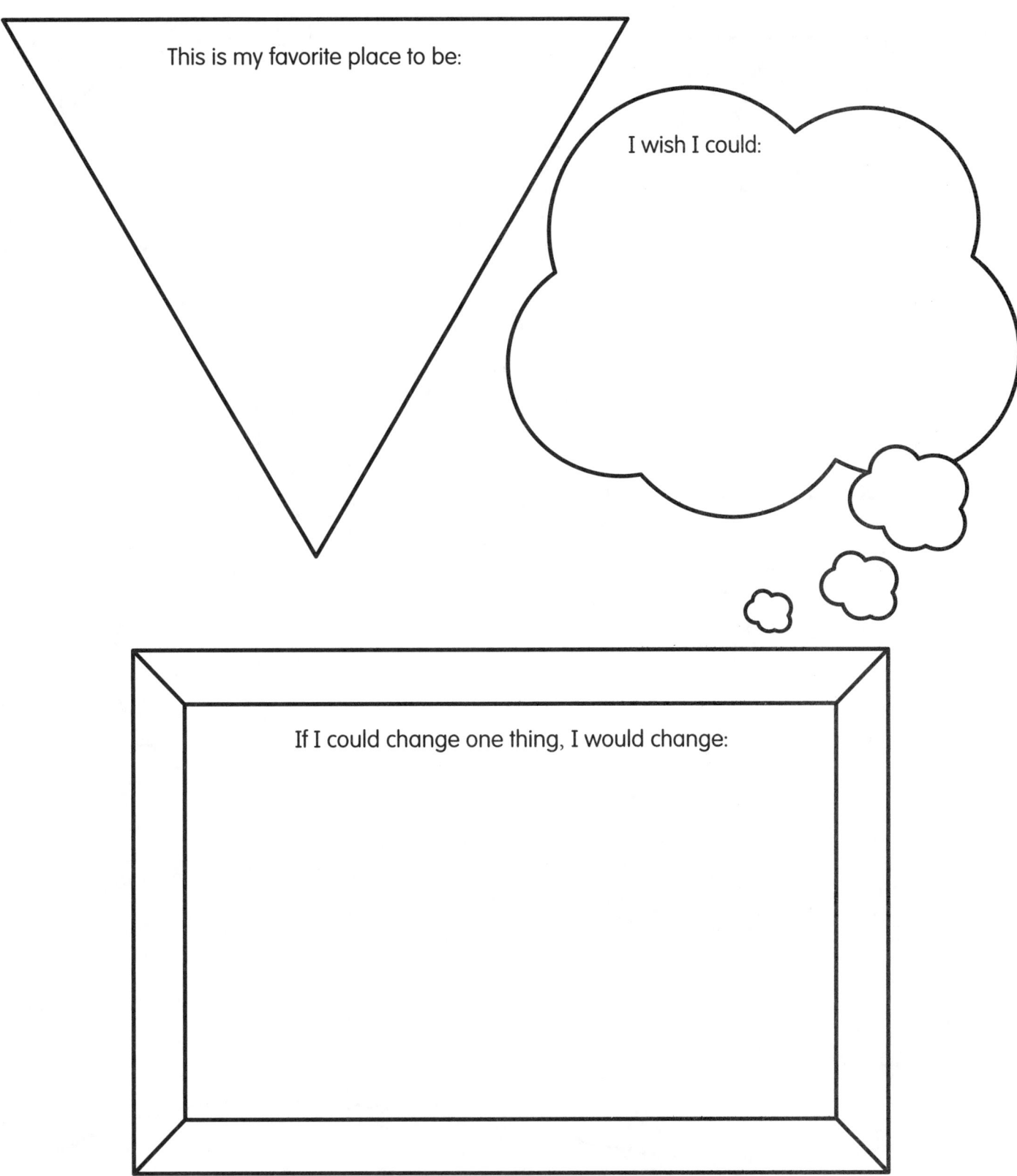

This is my favorite place to be:

I wish I could:

If I could change one thing, I would change:

Class Book Name _____

About Me, *continued*

Draw and write to tell about you.

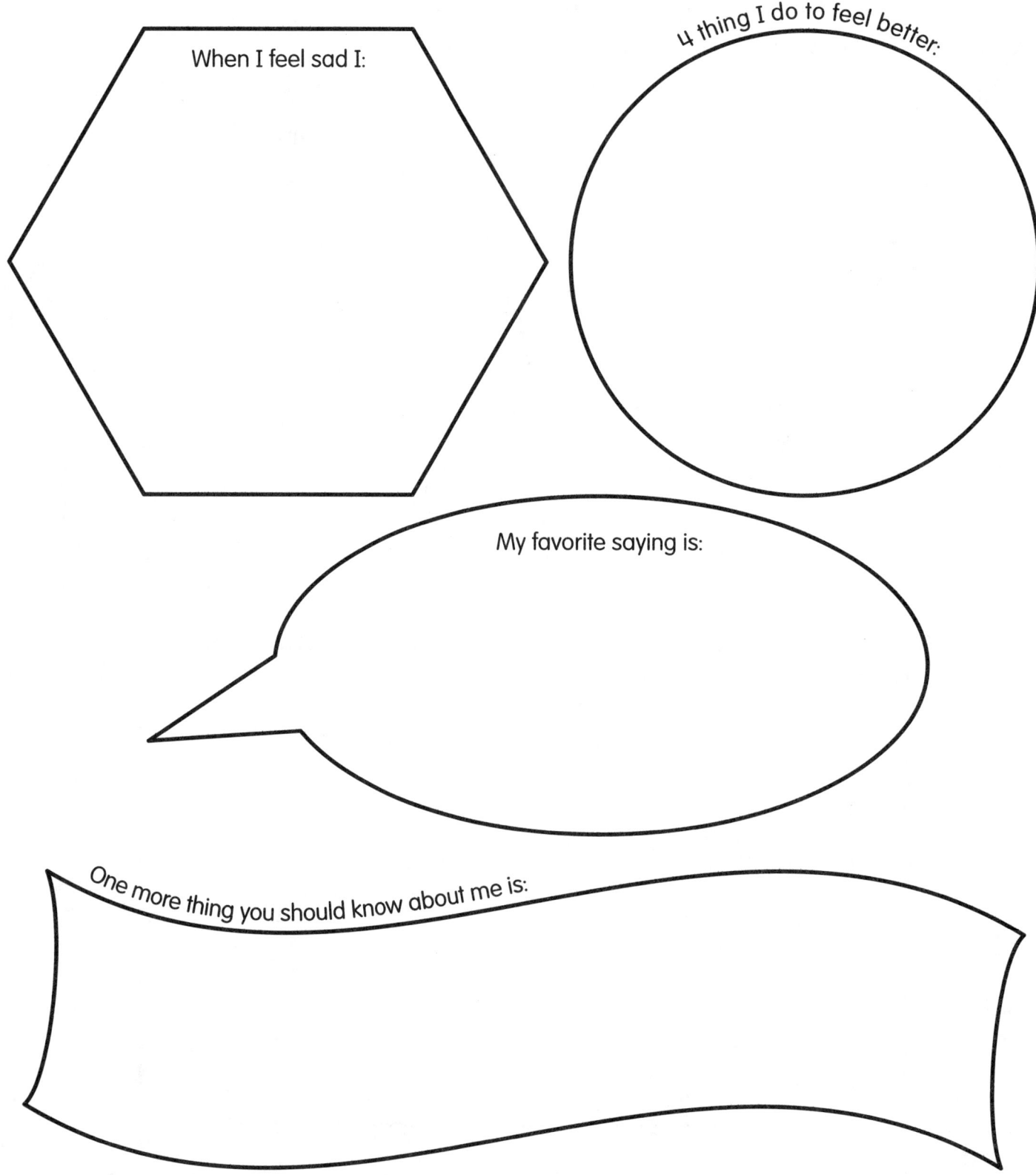

Class Book   Name _____

My Family's Culture

Your family's culture is the traditions, habits, and values your family has. It's who you are as a family. Mark the box to show which things are part of your family's culture. Then write a few details about it. Write anything that is missing from the list in the last two boxes.

☐ holidays	
☐ celebrations	
☐ special foods	
☐ sports	
☐ religion	
☐ music, singing	
☐ exercise	
☐ community service	
☐ watching movies together	
☐ making things together	
☐	
☐	

Class Book   Name _____

My Family's Culture, *continued*

Do you have parents, grandparents, or family members who express their culture or cultures through the kinds of foods they make or the kinds of foods they eat? Talk to your family members and get the recipes from them. Write them on the recipe cards.

Recipe _____

From the
kitchen of _____

Drawing of the food

🍴 **Ingredients:**   🍴 **Directions:**

_____   _____
_____   _____
_____   _____
_____   _____

Recipe _____

From the
kitchen of _____

Drawing of the food

🍴 **Ingredients:**   🍴 **Directions:**

_____   _____
_____   _____
_____   _____
_____   _____

Class Book

Name _____

My Family's Culture, *continued*

Language is part of culture. Does your family speak a different language at home than what you usually speak at school? Write and draw to tell about it.

My family speaks this language: _____

My family members come from these countries or places:

[   ]

Cultural symbols can be flags, statues, colors, or a certain way of dressing.
A cultural symbol has meaning to the people from that culture.
Draw 2 cultural symbols below from your family's culture or cultures.

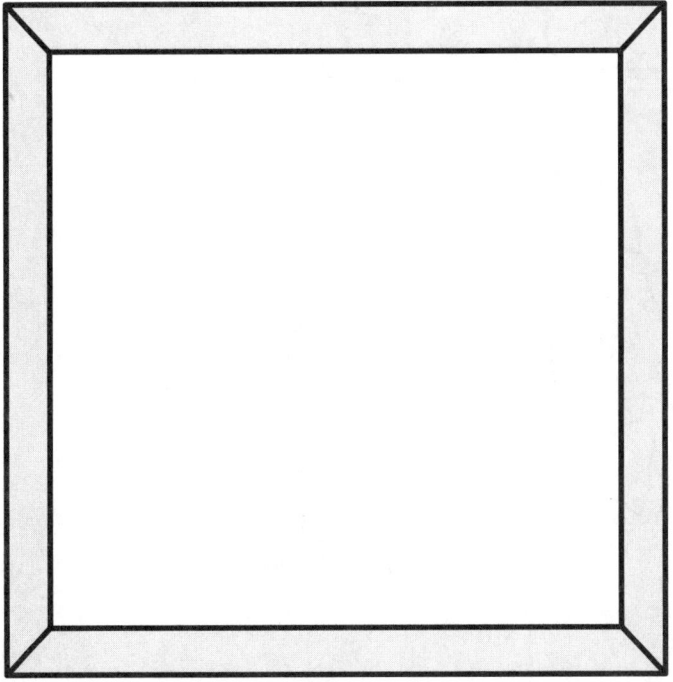 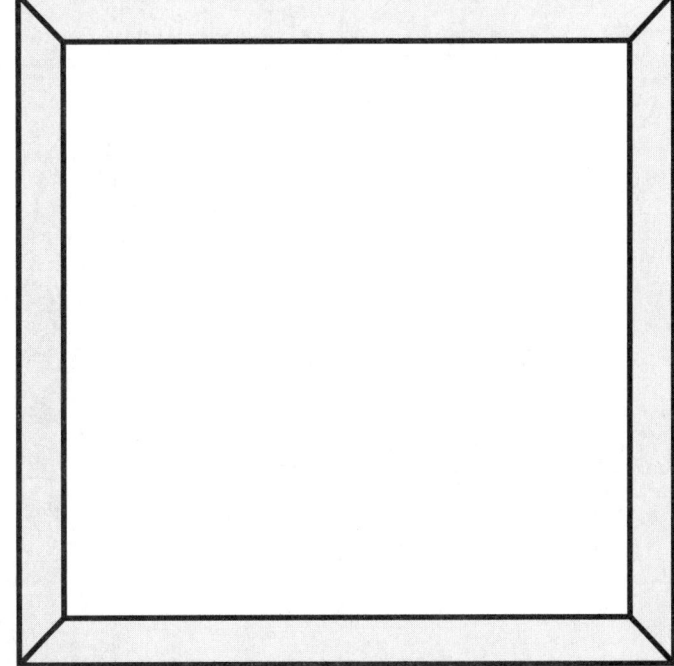

Class Book

My Name Page

Color the letters of your name. Then cut them out and spell your name. Glue your name to a sheet of construction paper. Were you named after someone? Does your name have a special meaning? Write to tell about it below your name.

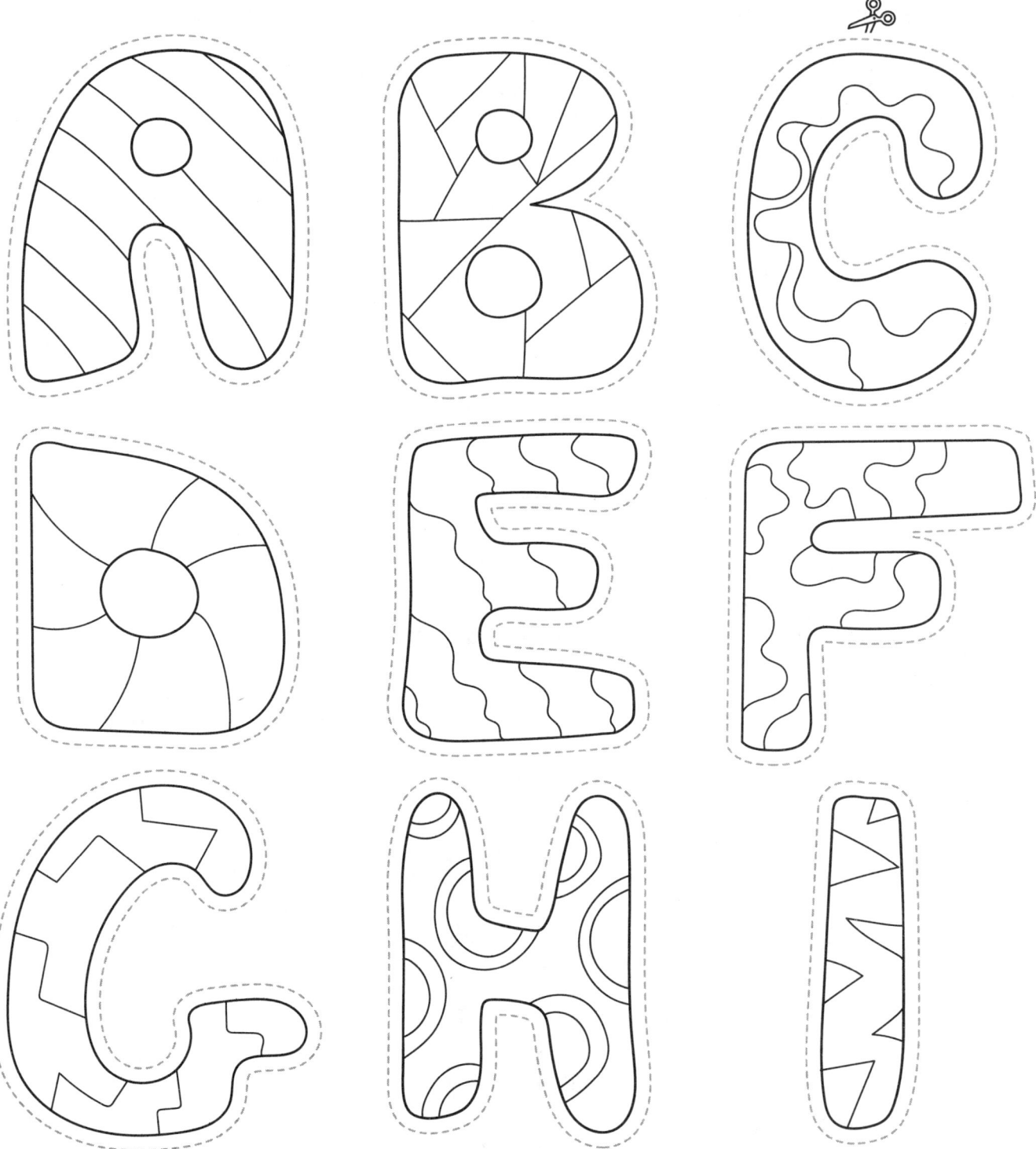

140   Culturally Responsive Lessons and Activities • EMC 8266 • © Evan-Moor Corporation

Class Book

My Name Page

Color the letters of your name. Then cut them out and spell your name. Glue your name to a sheet of construction paper. Were you named after someone? Does your name have a special meaning? Write to tell about it below your name.

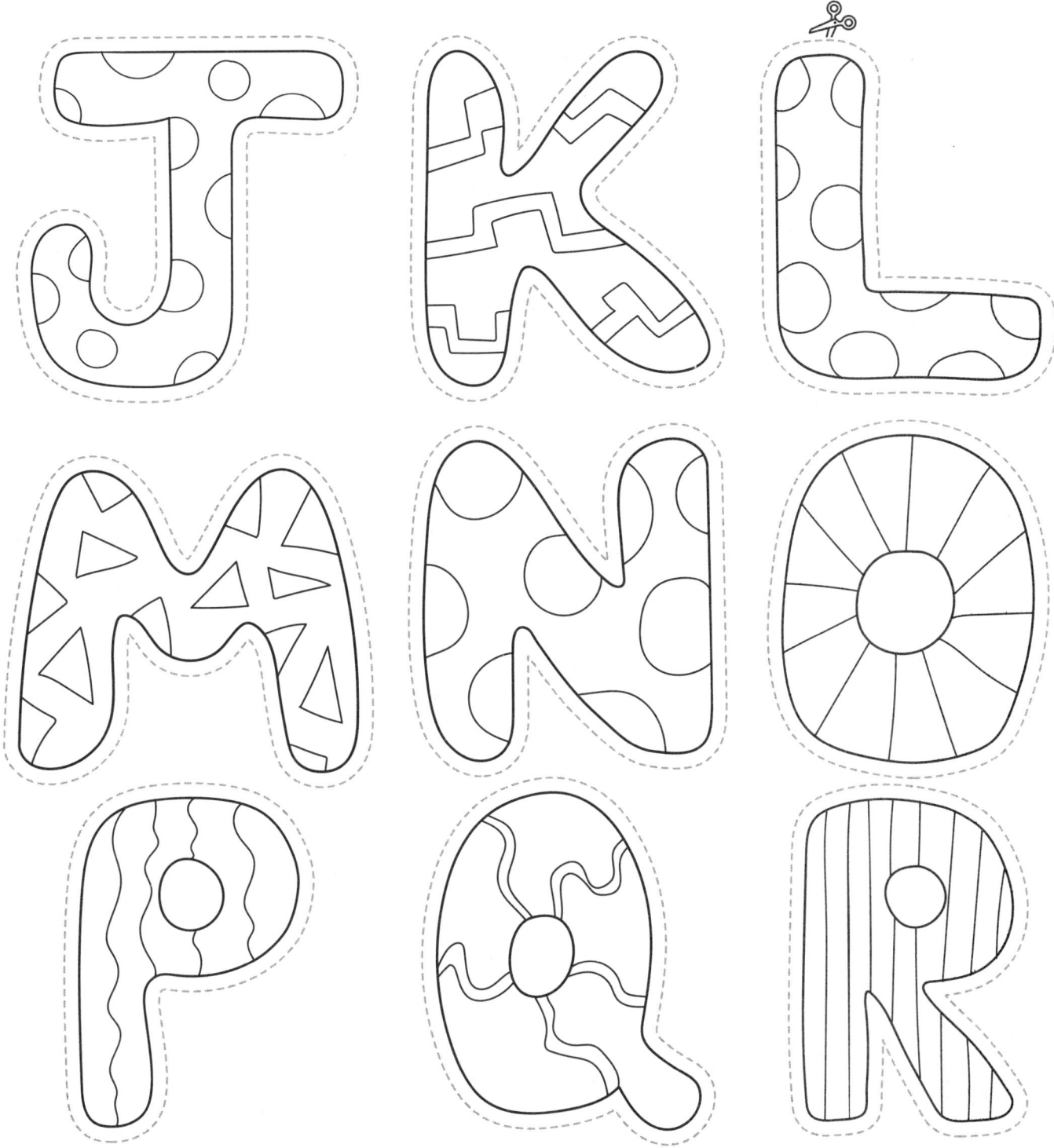

My Name Page

Color the letters of your name. Then cut them out and spell your name. Glue your name to a sheet of construction paper. Were you named after someone? Does your name have a special meaning? Write to tell about it below your name.

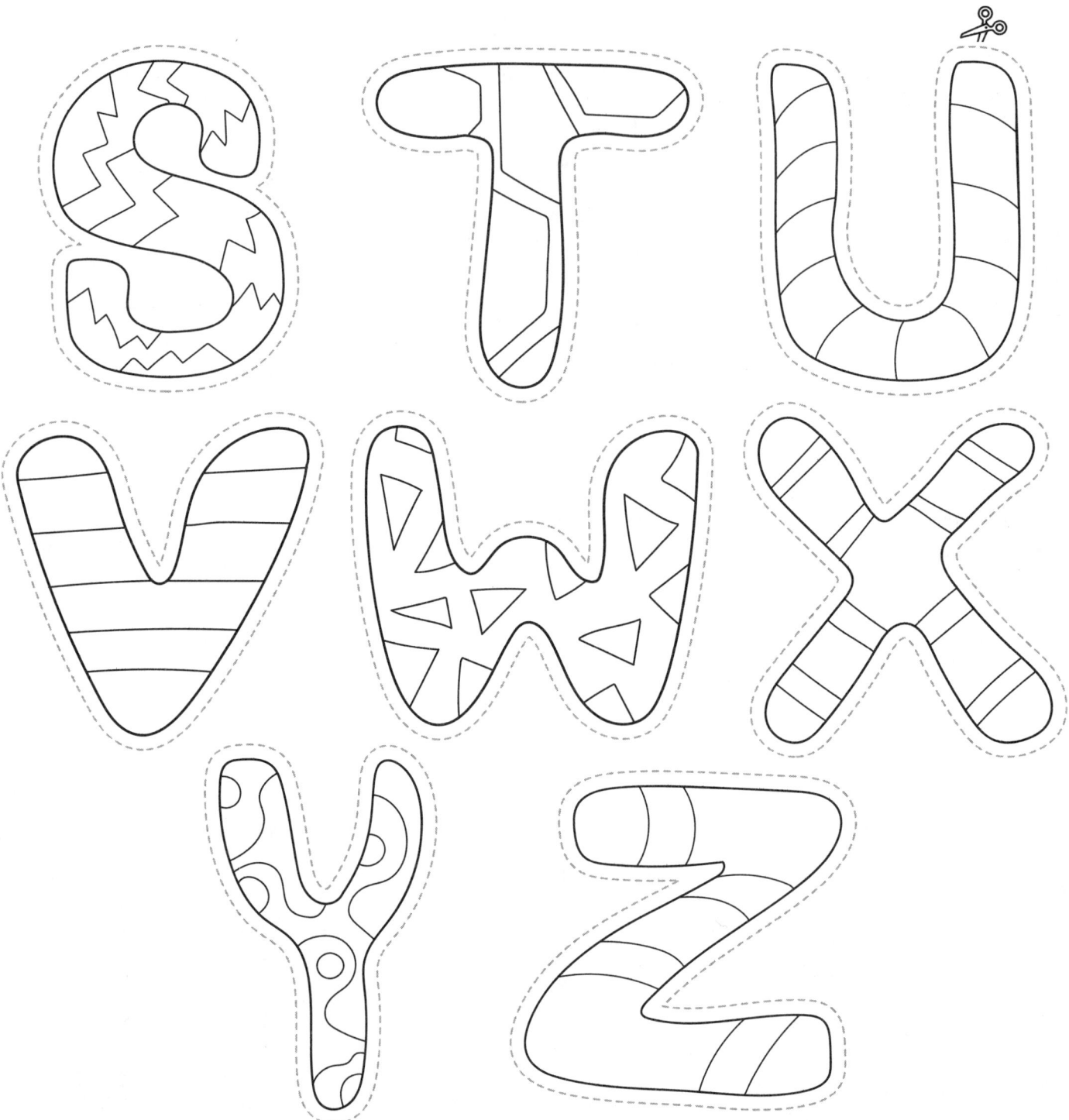

Class Book Name _____

My Photo or Picture

Ask someone to take a photo of you and help you print it. Then tape it in the square below. Or you can draw a picture of yourself in the square. Last, draw on and decorate the frame around the square.

Class Book

Name _____

My Dedication Page

You wrote pages for a class book. A lot of book authors write a dedication. A dedication page tells who the author wants to thank or show appreciation to. You can dedicate your book pages to people you care about or admire. You can dedicate your book pages to one person or multiple people.

Draw and write to tell whom you want to dedicate your book pages to.